I know I don't know you, but...

true stories, reflections and advice on divorce

HOLLY BELL

Beebowl Books

First published in Great Britain in 2021 by Beebowl Books

ISBN 978-1-9168729-0-5

A CIP catalogue record of this book is available in the British Library.

Printed and bound in England.

Cover artwork by Holly Bell
Proofreader: Victoria Cordell
Copyeditors: Nicky Lovick
Production manager: Joe Simpson

Foreword

I never thought I'd get divorced. Who does?

I entered into my marriage with youthful exuberance and a positivity which was probably insufferable to friends. I really did believe that when you make a promise that something is forever, you should mean it, and, hence, make it happen. I had heard being married could be hard work, but, honestly, I felt people who said that had either a) married the wrong person or b) were being dramatic. I didn't have much sympathy for tales of marital misery.

And then divorce happened to me. Or rather, I chose divorce. And I blushed at my younger, less-experienced view on marriage. When I told people what was happening, that my marriage was coming to an end, I was surprised by their responses. Mums I barely knew in the playground wanted to talk to me, friends confessed their marriages were deeply unhappy, women I'd never met in real life sent me long messages on social media about their own divorces and experiences. I became the 'divorced friend' who was suggested as a coffee date to other newly separated women. And I found myself often sympathising, sometimes sharing what I had done in their situation, and, when asked, I gave advice. Sometimes I gave advice even when it wasn't requested. More on that later.

The messages mushroomed though. It became hard to manage. I've been shocked, surprised and humbled by the volume of women who have contacted me, telling me their stories, asking for advice, giving me advice, wanting to just reach out to say that we have a shared experience. Mainly, wanting to be heard.

And through all this, I realised that there wasn't any one place that the collective wisdom of divorced women was shared. Sure, there were books about the legalities of divorce. There were books on starting again after divorce. There were memoirs, too. But there wasn't an all-encompassing book; a book a bit like a friend who would advise you on what to do with your wedding ring as well as how to move forward without feeling the years you spent married were wasted time.

So here it is. This isn't a 'you go, girl!' rallying cry to divorcees. It's not a sentimental collection of stories. Or a legal handbook with template letters to send to your ex. It's pithier. Divorced women don't have time on their hands for long, meandering essays. They're taking their second chance with both hands. Because we haven't got time to waste, have we?

And the title. It's the way many women started the conversation with me. 'I know I don't know you, but…' was their ice breaker. And now I am borrowing it to break the ice with you.

Introduction

No two separations are the same. No two divorces identical. So this book will never be all-encompassing. But I do know, from listening to so many women's stories, that there are recurring themes. And there are lessons to be passed on which could help anyone, whether you left or your ex left, whether you were cheated on, did the cheating or maybe just grew apart. I hope it helps.

Warning

This book contains explicit and possibly triggering content including details of domestic violence, psychological abuse, emotional abuse, neglect and trauma. Please read with caution if you feel you may become distressed from reading about these subjects.

How the book works

I've ordered the chapters into groups so that if you want to read about narcissism, it's all in one place, the same for going to court, children etc. It's very hard to write about divorce in a linear way, as often situations happen in different orders for different people. I also wanted you to be able to read it in small, snatched moments. When I was going through my divorce my mind wasn't able to cope with following long narratives. It was jumpy and easily distracted. So short chapters it is.

You'll notice that 'abuse' and 'narcissism' are split into two chapters. Being in a relationship with someone with Narcissistic Personality Disorder (NPD) is, of course, an abusive experience, but crucially not all abusers have NPD, so I have split them up. However, if you feel that either chapter is useful to you, it may be worth reading both of them.

Contents

Chapter 1

The End of the Marriage

It Takes Two

I was asked to be godmother by one of my oldest friends. Things had been very difficult in my marriage in the months before the ceremony. I'd made a pact with myself to really try and make things work between us; one big, final push to save things. The night before the baptism, he'd done what he always did whenever there was a big event that didn't revolve around him; he went out, got drunk and turned his phone off. I of course, as usual, stayed up waiting for him to get home, imagining some harm had come to him. (It never had, unless you count the damage to his liver.) He could barely walk when he finally rolled through the door at 3.30am. I told him I hated him and he looked at me, squinted a bit and said 'you deserve a slap', then turned around, opened the wardrobe door and urinated in it. I didn't sleep much; I felt like we'd gone to a place we couldn't come back from. In the morning we trudged to the church, silently, the kids chattering away oblivious. During the service when the priest said 'and now we offer each other the sign of peace' and everyone shook hands with the people next to them, I looked at my husband and thought how I felt no peace towards the man I married, because he didn't bring peace. I didn't want to shake his hand. I didn't want to call a truce. In fact, I felt more peace and kindness towards every stranger in that church than I did towards him. It finally dawned on me that our marriage couldn't work if only I was making any effort. It was my epiphany moment. Jenny, 43.

There's a point in every flailing marriage when one person, the one who wants the marriage to last more than the other, decides to really try and make it work. They almost make a pact with themselves. That they will do everything in their power to save it, and they wonder if perhaps one person's effort could be gargantuan enough to make up for another's lack.

This could entail anything and everything; cooking their favourite meals and laying the table beautifully, ensuring the children are asleep by the time they come home, listening intently to their work tales, learning to fish, agreeing to buy the dog they wanted, booking exciting weekend trips to European cities, encouraging them to go to the pub with their mates every night, attending a butchery class together, doing that thing they like in bed more often, inviting their friends over for a barbecue despite them not being your kind of people…essentially whatever floats their boat.

Whatever you end up doing to save the marriage, if only one of you is making this effort, it will in time make you feel even more miserable than before. None of the efforts listed are wrong (to each their own), but when you watch how much happier your spouse becomes through your efforts, you start to realise how much happier you could be if they cared enough to do the same. It really does take two to make a marriage.

Behind Every Criticism is a Wish

Our son was born on the same day as his best friend's birthday. When I saw my due date fell around this time I shuddered and hoped the baby wouldn't be born on Neil's birthday, because I had a horrible feeling Neil would still be more important to him than our baby. I was gutted when I went into labour the day before. He left the maternity hospital after Jamie was born and went straight out on the lash with Neil. And so began years of preferring to celebrate with Neil over Jamie. There was always an excuse; first it was that Jamie was so young he wouldn't notice, then it was that Jamie would prefer to be with his mates than his dad. I would nag him about it, make bitchy comments. I didn't know how to tackle it head on because it took my breath away that he preferred to be with his mates over his family. Eventually I stopped nagging and for me that was a big marker that I had stopped caring. In the end I found a man who wanted to be with me and Jamie on his birthday, despite Jamie not being his own flesh and blood. And I don't nag him, because he's lovely. JoJo, 37.

I hate the word 'nag' for obvious reasons. A word to describe (usually) a woman, pulling up (usually) a man on poor behaviour. I always think of nagging as a way through which women make criticism more palatable.

In a previous life I worked in advertising and had to manage and appraise members of staff. I noticed that to make people feel better about criticism I was feeding back, I'd playfully suggest I was a nag. So instead of 'it's been noted that you're not copy checking adverts before they go to press and clients have complained about typos', I'd say, 'Look, I know I nag about this, but you really must copy check thoroughly as clients don't like it when ads go to press with typos!', followed by a laugh. I had learnt through society and imitating other female managers that nagging went down better than direct criticism.

In a marriage 'nagging' has real intention, just like it does in an office. It's a criticism of behaviour, behind which is a wish. If you have found yourself nagging, bitching, criticising, whatever you want to call it, think about what the wish is behind the criticism. For JoJo she wished that her husband cared more about his son than his best friend. It was that simple. Strip back all the other noise and think about what your wishes are and if the person you are married to is willing or able to fulfil them. This is especially helpful when you are considering if the marriage is salvageable.

Anger

I was angry throughout my marriage. Not with my husband. I was angry with myself. Angry for choosing him and getting it so wrong. Angry for not thinking more about what a dreadful match it was. So ill-fitting. The anger internalised so that I ate myself to a size 22, I drank too much, too often and was regularly 'that' drunk friend on a night out. It spilled out as well; I was a furious person, regularly screaming and beeping my horn as I drove to work. I have a lot of shame over some of my behaviour. I wasn't very nice, just filled with fury. Gracie, 52.

I slammed more car doors when I was married than I have before and after in total. In fact, I don't think I have slammed a car door since I divorced. When I was married, fury was within me, bubbling away. This is not a criticism of my ex-husband, it's simply a fact. It took me almost nine years to examine where that internalised anger came from, but, once I saw it, I couldn't ignore it.

What can you do if you feel like this? Okay, well, first you need to forgive yourself for the anger you've directed inwards. There's no other way to move forward. Any therapist will tell you that internalising rage is a very female occupation. When you're furious, the emotion has to go somewhere. Whether you've overeaten, undereaten, self-harmed, drunk too much, shouted at the kids, been a pain to work with, put yourself in risky situations; let it go. If you need professional help, seek it.

For the anger you've directed outwards; you have choices. Obviously you can't track down all the people you've impatiently honked your horn at, but you can be a kind and considerate driver from now on. For the family and friends who you might owe an apology to, swallow your pride and do it. Properly, without blaming. Say you are truly sorry for how you behaved and expect nothing in return for the apology. It's freeing.

Then have a think about what it was that induced that rage. The theme I hear again and again from women is not feeling known by their husband, and that being a truly lonely place to be. Choosing to be alone through divorce can feel way less lonely than being unknown in a marriage.

<u>The Tapping</u>

It's hard to pinpoint when it started, but it got louder. There was this nagging sensation that this wasn't the life I was supposed to lead. I felt like I was playing a role in a play instead of living an authentic life. I remember on our honeymoon watching him try to order a coffee in French and failing. Instead of asking me for help, he just repeated his order louder and louder to the waiter. I was on my honeymoon with a Brit Abroad and I thought how this really wasn't what I liked or wanted, but that the honeymoon was a bit soon to be finding fault, so put it to the back of my mind. That nagging sensation kept coming back though. When he bought himself a present for our second daughter's birth and didn't get me anything, the nagging feeling was deafening. I knew I'd chosen the wrong man. Charlotte, 39.

There comes a point in every marriage where this pesky little inner truth-teller taps you on the shoulder to alert you that all is not as it should be. You will likely ignore it. That's okay. We've all turned a blind eye to painful truths. The question is, how long you will be able to do this? Some women travel through their entire life in a marriage that lacks authenticity. Some even go into a marriage knowing it's wrong: maybe they marry for money, maybe they marry for social status, maybe they marry because they simply didn't have the heart to say no and disappoint their partner. (Though this might be a particularly British affliction.) Most of us, though, enter into marriage with the best of intentions, but, like many a destination, it turns out to be a little different to what we imagined.

I call this 'the tapping'. Most of us can't ignore it forever, that all is not as it should be. We may try and anaesthetise through antidepressants, or flavoured gins, or perhaps obsessing over the school careers of our children, or aggressive PTA activity, or yoga, or eating clean or literal cleaning; polluting the house with floral disinfectant can be very distracting, or, or, or, maybe an affair, if we can find someone discreet and willing. But the very problem with any problem, is that you carry it with you. No matter how busy you keep the internal chatter to distract yourself, when the silence falls, it's just you and your problem. Wherever you go, you take the tapping with you.

These tappings can be daily or yearly or anything in between. It could be the time you insisted you could smell something cidery and rotting in your house to be gaslit and told you were imagining things, only months later to discover putrid gifted Bramley apples under the stairs. It might be the refusal to come and visit your mother in hospital after a stroke because, well, their ex's aunt survived hers. It might be making you stand up and be measured at a Boxing Day lunch, to prove their point that you are not tall; your height is a fabrication. It might be the lover's gifts with pet names hidden in the shed, carefully pushed behind the paddling pool, but not quite hidden well enough. It might be their refusal to kiss you on the mouth. It might be the shaving of their pubic hair despite you finding the plucked chicken look unattractive. It might be that they never make a sound when you have sex; you wonder if you could simply be a vessel for them to deposit in. It might be that they had to be woken up to witness their children being born. It might be the lack of celebration of your triumphs.

These are all real-life examples from women who have written to me about the darker times of their marriage, the tapping on the shoulder moments. When you finally listen to the tapping and face it head on, you realise that at the heart of every divorce is a desire to tell the truth, a deep-seated need to live authentically. Whether you're the one to do the leaving or you're the one who is left, at the core of the unrest is that one or both of you are not being entirely honest about your marriage. And guess what? It turns out, an authentic life feels like peace.

<u>Listening</u>

I was forever last on the list. I would ask him to look after the boys whilst I went for a run, but he always had an excuse as to why he couldn't. Then he was suddenly training for an Ironman competition and out every evening. I didn't have the energy to argue with him and point out how unfair this was. I came to dread Christmas; I used to buy and wrap all the presents for everyone, including myself! One Christmas morning he watched as the boys unwrapped their stockings and he whispered to me, 'I love this, it's as much a surprise to me as it is to them.' He thought this was funny, but to me it felt so sad. He kind of opted out of family life and watched on instead. In the end I had an affair. I have a lot of guilt over it, but I just always felt last on the list. I wanted him to care about me and love me and be involved in our family, but he was always too busy on his phone, or cycling or gaming. My new partner is actually a willing participant in our relationship and I finally feel I know the true meaning of the word 'partner'. We are a team. Izzy, 35.

Even the best listeners don't always pay attention to the more covert methods of communication. You might pride yourself on being someone who listens with care and compassion to your friend's problems. You are present when your children tell you about their latest friendship struggle; you're no phone scroller. You are excellent at taking feedback at work and using it to improve.

But do you listen to the way people treat you? Not what they say, what they do. Because, without wanting to come over all self-help book, love is a verb. Moreover, kindness is a verb. Respect is a verb. And if you don't listen to how someone treats you and act upon it, beware the perils.

It might be a small thing, or seemingly small. Perhaps it is the division of labour for Christmas? You fantasise about making a list together, dividing and conquering. It would be fun! But no, they're too busy for that, work is slammed at the moment, and then there's the triathlon they're training for, and their old band mates have planned a weekend reunion away, and...you get the idea.

There's a reason why a significant other is called a 'partner' – they should truly be your partner, not someone who is too busy, too important, too tired, too *anything* to participate fully and equally in an event that means something to your family. This applies to birthdays, holidays, Christmas etc., but also the washing, the cleaning, the money earning, the child rearing. If *they aren't willing to engage with the things that are important to you, and if you have made this clear, and they still aren't interested in working as a team, and* crucially it bothers you – *and* crucially it makes you unhappy, then listen to what your spouse is saying by refusing to engage and participate.

I'll spell it out; if the above is true for you, your spouse is telling you that their time/happiness is more important than anyone else's. Especially yours. Listen. Please listen! People are really, in general, not as complicated as they might seem. Most are front and centre exactly what they show you. As the saying goes, if it looks like a duck, quacks like a duck and walks like a duck – it is indeed a duck. Or rather, if your spouse acts like an arsehole, they are an arsehole.

Treating someone poorly is catching. It's a long and disappointing game to raise children in a household where your spouse treats you with silent contempt (or indeed worse), only to receive the same from your sons when they come of age. Or even worse, to watch your daughters become pathologically addicted to partners who are emotionally distant, even abusive. This rotting spreads through families and down generations. Admittedly, it's very scary to put a stop to it. Whether through calling it out and asking for change or ending a marriage in more serious cases.

As soon as you stop allowing yourself to come last on the list, if your partner isn't willing to change, the writing will be on the wall for your marriage.

<u>The Straw</u>

I know it sounds trivial, but I called time on my marriage over a frame. I'd had a photo of the children framed professionally six months previously as a gift for his birthday. It sat propped up against the wall all that time. I asked him to hang it more than once and he made excuses. Then I suggested I do it. He didn't like that idea. Next, I suggested I pay for someone to come in and do it. That was a no too. In the end, one of the kids knocked it over and the glass cracked. It said so much to me that he couldn't find the time to hang a frame, but always had time for the pub on a Friday with his mates and watching TV shows about cars. I told him I wasn't happy and it escalated from there. Mollie, 33.

The straw is the very thing that springs you into action. Now it might be your spouse sitting you down and telling you they're in love with someone else. (Though I do know of some women who have tolerated this and suggested everyone just carry on and ignore the mistress-shaped elephant in the room. To each their own, but I have always been a jealous type.)

The straw could be more one of those 'tapping' moments described on page 5. And if you're the one calling the shots, there will be that final straw moment when everything rushes through your head, cinematically, and you'll see the marriage for what it is, and decide there and then that it is over. You may not tell them in that moment, but you will always, always remember it. It will be a moment you dine out on, that you tell many a newly separated woman about in solidarity. And they will share their moment too.

The straw can be trivial, seemingly. But it is about what they signify. I know a woman who left her husband because he only liked to eat frozen peas with his dinner. No other veg would do. Not even fresh peas. The woman in question did not have anything against frozen peas of course, it was what this fixation represented; her husband's narrow world of experience and refusal to experiment with anything alien. There was a whole world (of vegetables) out there and she gave herself permission to be set free and explore.

The straw can be something very serious though. A slap. A punch. A humiliation. The more I am told of individual last straws, the more I can see they reflect the Achilles heel of the person on the receiving end. For me, being ignored is my red mist trigger, and says more about me than any therapist might be able to eke out. For at the centre of who I am, there is a little girl who is desperate to be heard and acknowledged. Being ignored is a deal-breaker for me. Never mind any other unhappiness. Oh no. Being ignored trumps everything.

<u>Cheating</u>

We went to a 30th birthday party in a huge field. It was beautiful. There was a circus-type tent, a wood-fired pizza van, homemade sloe gin, you get the idea. I was so looking forward to it. When we arrived, I saw a beautiful, quite drunk girl in a stunning blue dress. I knew what would happen. Sure enough he disappeared for 40 minutes, as did Blue Dress Girl, only to return and immediately accuse me of flirting with a friend's husband. I knew what he'd done. I asked him where he'd been and he didn't even dignify me with a response, just stared at me. It was a good six months after we separated that the friend whose party it'd been called me and said how embarrassed she'd been about what had happened with Blue Dress Girl. My instinct had been spot on. Mary, 34.

It matters not who cheated. Listen again, before you say 'but he…' It matters not. As a good friend of mine said: 'blaming the person who did it is mindless, an affair is a symptom'. It could be a symptom of being deeply unhappy in a marriage, a cry for help. It could be a symptom of being a total arsehole who doesn't care for the other party. It could be a symptom of a lack of physical affection that itches to the bone. It could be any and all of these things, and more, all mixed together. What it is, is a moment to re-evaluate. If you have cheated, take stock and think about what it means that you've looked outside your marriage. Affairs are rarely a crisis of the primary relationship, and more often a crisis of the self. If you have been cheated on, take the time to think about whether this relationship you are in is right for you. See it as a gift. It's very, very painful to be betrayed, for sure. Finding out you've been cheated on tramples on your heart so badly you feel it won't ever recover. (It will.) Some truths really do break your heart but fix your vision, as the saying goes.

And if your spouse is the one who strayed, never ever ask them for details of the sex they had. That way madness lies. It's hard when you're imagining moments of intense pleasure between the person you love and another, but really, sex is sex. It can be tender and sexy and magical and filmic. Though all at the same time, it can be smelly and awkward and squelchy and farty and animal.

The Script

I look back now and realise there were some serious red flags that he was having an affair. The main thing was that he couldn't stop talking about her! He's a stay-at-home dad and suddenly every other sentence was about Carrie. We couldn't even have a conversation about recycling without him bringing it back to Carrie. That and his newfound attachment to his phone. It went everywhere with him. Password changed, phone taken into the bathroom for showers etc. I asked him about it more than once and was told I was being insane. I even found a present from her he'd hidden, but he said I was reading into things too much. In the end, after so many confrontations, he admitted he was in love with Carrie. He said she didn't know. To cut a long story short, over a year later, I asked him to leave and he finally admitted they had been sleeping together all along. Now I am divorcing him and he is being a total prick. Really difficult and nasty despite my best efforts to keep everything friendly for the sake of the children. I wish he'd been straight with me, it would have been better for everyone. Gemma, 35.

I learnt about The Script from Mumsnet. It is the script that a lot of men follow when you start to suspect they are having an affair. I thought it was worth including in this book because from the tales I have been told by multiple women, it does seem to be quite common. So it goes a bit like this:

1. Your suspicion is wrong

You suspect he is having an affair because of 'mention-itis', phone possessiveness, his newfound love of the gym or need to buy new clothes. You ask him and he denies it, usually professing undying love and making you feel awful for even suspecting infidelity.

2. The evidence is wrong

You find evidence he is having an affair, from texts to hotel stays to stolen phone calls. You confront him with the evidence and he denies it, usually in an angry fashion.

3. The proof is wrong, and, furthermore, you are insane

You expend huge amounts of energy and time obtaining proof of the affair. Once you have it you sit him down and present your case. He denies it again and often accuses you of being mad.

4. It was only emotional

You feel that you can't trust him anymore, are incensed that he can't even level with you when faced with evidence, so you tell him to leave. This triggers a confession that yes there is someone else but nothing has happened, it's just an emotional affair and that he's very confused. At this point he seems to want sympathy for being puzzled by his own feelings.

5. Actually, scrap that, she's the love of my life

After spending some time away from the family home for a bit, he tries to come back. You refuse, as you're still pretty sure there's some major lying going on. Then the admission that, yes, he is having an affair and yes he is in love with her and, to add insult to injury, he never loved you anyway. (Somewhat reminiscent of a toddler when they fall out with their playmate?)

6. How dare you divorce me, you're evil

Given you are now in possession of all the information, that there was indeed an affair all along, that apparently he has never loved you and that now he is off to live the life he always wanted with his lover, you issue divorce proceedings. Then all hell breaks loose. You are breaking up the family, you are making this deliberately difficult, you are jealous of their deep love, you are evil, you need to stop trying to ruin his life.

7. This isn't what I thought it would be, remember what we had together?

Reality bites after six months to two years with the new love of his life and he starts to realise that she's not as great as he thought. He gets back in contact. It's all been a terrible mistake and actually he loves you really, it was always you. Can he come back? Please? He chooses you after all!

The Script can be re-run many times. It's not always a one-time-only drama. It can be replayed with the same affair partner, or with different ones each time. The relationship board of Mumsnet is awash with varying iterations of The Script. It makes for depressing reading. Not so much the amount of men having affairs, more the amount of women being gaslit (see page 148).

I have my own theories about The Script. I think for a lot of men who follow it, the slow and gradual reveal of an affair is the only way they can accept their own behaviour.

I have witnessed relationships that have survived affairs, but it's always where The Script does not feature. Marriages can survive infidelity but trying to make someone think they're losing their mind to protect the ego, well, that's hard to come back from.

Private Detectives

I found myself obsessed with catching him in the act. He'd joined a gym, lost weight, started to dress better. His phone never left his side, the office suddenly needed him to work late. I knew. But for some reason I had to have evidence. I don't know what I thought, that I was going to take him to some kind of infidelity court and present my case? A friend offered to follow him but I felt it was too risky. So I hired a private detective. They put a tracker on his car, apparently it's completely legal…who knew? Anyway, they caught him with a woman he worked with. I wasted a lot of money confirming something I already knew. Betty, 35.

You think you need proof of their infidelity? Nope, you really don't. If you're at the point where you genuinely feel you need to have them followed because you don't trust them or their reporting of what they've been doing, things are pretty terminal. Trust is everything. Save your money and spend it on legal fees.

Gilded Cages

I'm an actress and have been in some pretty big films. I get recognised regularly; I guess you could say I'm famous. I watched Prince William and Kate get married from a very expensive hotel room I was staying in for work. I found myself sobbing tears of foreboding. I looked at them and thought, 'God, you have no idea how bad it can be.' I kept thinking how everyone would think their marriage is perfect, but actually fame and money don't make for a happy marriage. I should know. Money is no shield. Or fame. I actually think it can make the cage of marriage harder to leave. Your livelihood depends on people's perception of you and if part of that is being in a happy marriage, you're stuck in whatever marriage you have, happy or not. I say yes to films I don't even like just to make more money, so that I can work towards leaving. It's actually quite good to have a focus. M, 46.

You might think M's story doesn't apply to us mere mortals, but I think it does. That gilded cage doesn't have to be one where the paparazzi are outside and the pay cheque has six figures. The gilded cage might be a three-bed semi, a second-hand people carrier and being the mum who always helps with the second-hand uniform sale at the school. It's the world you inhabit and the perception others have of you because of it. Whatever the cage is that you're used to, stepping out into the unknown can feel very scary. It's okay to be scared of the unknown. And though it might sound trite, the unknown is only unknown until you cross its threshold.

The Rehearsal

Once I decided it was over, I couldn't get him out the house fast enough. I wanted it done. I think in hindsight I was a bit too brutal. The thing is I'd lived with the thought of divorce for some time and come to terms with what it would mean. I forgot he hadn't. I told him it was over and expected him to be at the stage I was at, but of course he wasn't. He was completely blindsided and acted like a wounded animal. I have a lot of regrets about it now, as I think my approach wasn't exactly conducive to a smooth separation. If I could do it again, I would be kinder, slower, gentler. Fiona, 47.

When you're the one ending the marriage, once you've hit the wall and The Straw (page 8) has been and gone, it can be very tempting to push forward and rip the plaster off. You rehearse and rehearse the moment where you state your case for a divorce. (Unlikely that these rehearsals factor in your spouse's response.) It all feels clean at this point. You envisage a Chris Martin/Gwyneth Paltrow-style conscious uncoupling, helping each other out when dating, maybe you might all be able to hang out together… Stop right now. These are fantasies.

Very few couples will be able to maintain a close friendship post-divorce. With that in mind you need to prepare. Live with the decision alone a little. Think about the steps you would take if you knew you would never see your spouse again. If they dropped off the face of the earth tomorrow, what would you wish you had done to prepare? For the person you know right now, that man you made vows with, maybe whose babies you grew in your body, from the moment you tell him it's over, he is no longer the same version of the man you married.

In just the same way that every child experiences how they are parented differently to their sibling, so too must you accept that your (ex) husband will change on his own terms from the moment you call it a day, for he stops being 'yours' from that moment. The implications of this are both practical and emotional.

Think about it – is the internet provider account in his sole name? The man you knew when you were married would never refuse to sign this over to you, would he? He would never be so cruel and punitive. Well, prepare to possibly be surprised. The father of your children wouldn't invade your privacy (would he?) and hack into your social media accounts? Not when he was the one who cheated? Consider changing your passwords on every single thing (to something he won't guess). You agreed the house would be signed over to you, without any buying-out cash exchanged? Get it in writing and signed off in court. People change their minds, especially when they meet a new partner.

To be very clear: they are not *your* husband from that split second you tell them it's over. And hurt can make people do some out-of-character things. So prepare for battle and in the event that your husband is kind and wonderful post separation, well, what a lovely surprise. You really do see what people are made of when you divorce them.

Permission to Divorce

It took meeting a woman called Nicole on a hen do for me to feel like it was okay to get divorced. I'd never met anyone who was divorced who seemed happier than my married friends. Maybe I just have ridiculously happy couple friends, but my only examples of divorce didn't feel like a life I wanted. I've always been a bit of a follower and needed others to do things first. Meeting Nicole was life- changing. She was divorced and happy and stunning and just seemed really at peace. You know those people who have an energy to them that's magnetic? She was one of those. Meeting her and seeing her as a happy, divorced woman gave me the permission I needed to leave my marriage. Georgina, 34.

Obviously you don't need permission from anyone to divorce, not least from your actual husband! Despite what many people think, given the vernacular phrase 'they asked me for a divorce', you really don't need your spouse's permission to begin divorce proceedings. Whether they contest it is another thing, but we will come to that in the legal section. (And things are a-changing; the law- makers are finally realising that if one person wants out of a marriage, they really should just be able to leave. A marriage should be a willing contract between two people, not a prison with one key holder.)

What I'm talking about is making your peace with the possibility of being a divorcee. For many of us (myself included) there is still some degree of shame in having been divorced. It's a badge of failure; a very public sharing of just how unlovable you are. It's a club that nobody ever enters into marriage thinking they would be a member of. I certainly never thought there'd be a folder in my email account called 'Divorce'.

I think part of my own feelings of shame were linked to my previous somewhat smug and judgemental opinions about others who divorced. I always saw it as a sign that they just didn't try hard enough. They'd taken the easy way out. We all know that marriage is hard at times, tough even, I felt that I soldiered through my own marriage like a warrior. I had battle scars that might never fully heal, but what mattered was that I was still married. I was a sticker, a stayer, a finisher, a mother who put her kids first. I wouldn't put my own happiness above the happiness of the children. And their happiness meant staying married, so married I stayed.

And, my goodness, I was good at it. I was the poster girl for smiling and giving advice on other people's relationships and setting up single friends, because, well, why would you not want to have a life like me (said through ever so slightly too firmly gritted smiling teeth). But I was a liar. I knew things weren't right, but I was too proud to admit it. I lied to everyone, including myself.

What I needed was permission to divorce. I needed someone I admired and thought brave and courageous to be my divorce pin-up. Role Model Divorcee, if you will. Nicole Kidman? I admired her breaking free, but she was too Hollywood for me to relate to. Maybe someone I knew? Except I didn't really know anyone who was divorced. Not anyone close.

I remember discussing my unhappiness with a friend once and babbling on about how to make the marriage better. I was incessantly talking. She stopped me and imparted some wisdom on me which I will never forget:

'Holly, you know divorce isn't the worst thing that can happen to a woman or to children. My mother and father divorced when I was very young and I really think it has been the making of me. It shaped me into who I am and I like who I am. You can get divorced and still have a happy ending.'

And do you know what? She was right. So please stop Googling exam results for children from single parent families, or prison statistics on children of divorce. Statistics are just that. You are you. Take permission from yourself to have a happier ending. And if you can't give yourself permission then I will give it to you. Here. Take it. It's yours.

<u>Things You Must Do Straight Away Which Are Boring</u>

Not long after he moved out, the girls went to his new flat for the weekend and took the family iPad with them in case they got bored. I completely forgot my email account was linked to the iPad and when they got back I realised he had looked at my emails which embarrassingly included an invoice email from Lovehoney for quite a few different vibrators. I felt really ashamed and could barely look him in the eye when I next saw him. And guess what? He played dirty and brought this up in court as 'evidence' of my reckless and selfish approach to money. Luckily it didn't seem to make any difference to the judge but I seriously wished the ground would swallow me up at the time. Esther, 30.

When you realise your marriage is ending, no matter how amicable, there are some very boring things you must do which will not feel like a priority at the time. But you must do them. If you need to, incentivise yourself to get them done with a reward at the end. And please don't think that because you and your ex are super-friendly and amicable at the moment, that it will always be like this. I hope it is for your sake, but, if it isn't, you'll be glad you did all these things:

1. Take copies/photos of any evidence of bank accounts (including the kids), savings, mortgages, stocks and shares, anything financial including the balances. If you have a prenup or a will, do the same. Send these to yourself so you have a copy online, then send them to a trusted friend or relative too, then put them in a third place.

2. Any evidence of poor behaviour (affairs, gambling addictions, abusive behaviour) take photos and do as above.

3. Change all your passwords on EVERYTHING to something they won't guess.

4. Disconnect any shared data apps such as Dropbox and if they are especially toxic, think about asking the school your children attend for individual app accounts for sharing homework, photos and other information.

5. Think about your home security. If you own the home together, you won't be able to legally change the locks until the home is solely in your name. If your ex has left and you are concerned they may try to get into your home, consider putting a chain on the inside of your front door to use when you are at home, and invest in a camera home video security system. Amazon sell reasonably priced ones and you can literally set it up to point from inside your house, through a window, at the front door. Exes can and do let themselves into the house after leaving and it's not a nice feeling to know that they might do this whenever they want. If you've been in an abusive relationship and are worried about your safety get some legal advice regarding getting an Occupation Order through the court.

6. Locate yours and your child/ren's passports and put them in a safe place. Make a note of the passport numbers and keep this separate too.

7. If you have a joint account or credit cards, speak to your bank/building society about what is best to do. You are still financially connected even after divorce until you are severed financially (a clean break). This is a separate process to getting a decree absolute. See the Legal chapter for more information, page 47.

8. Look at all direct debits and work out which bank account they come from so that you don't suddenly find yourself without the internet because he cancelled it, or with your mobile phone being cut off, or having your car being taken back by the hire company.

9. Speak to your children's schools discreetly to let them know what is going on. A lot of the pain of divorce is played out by children though their behaviour at school. It's better that they are aware and can support your children rather than think they're being a pain.

10. Arrange to speak to a solicitor for advice. It seems very expensive, but failing to get good legal advice is a fool's game. Be aware that once you consult a solicitor, they are unable to represent the other side. This is a tactic used by some unscrupulous people to stop their ex from getting good representation. They pay for an hour consultation with all the best solicitors within a radius and then watch as their ex has to engage someone from much farther afield, or worse, hires a less than brilliant firm.

11. Arrange an STI test. I'm not joking. If you have been left out of the blue and they insist there's no one else involved, it's highly likely this isn't true. It's also quite possible barrier protection has not been used.

12. Disable the Facebook memories thing and the 'on this day' photo reminder which iPhones helpfully send to you. Photos lie, they're a highlight reel. There is no photo of you rocking on the floor after they spoke to you like crap, no photo of the disappointment that they couldn't rouse themself from a nap to watch your baby being born...these things are not documented pictorially. But when you're feeling low, seeing a family photo with your ex in can lead to all kinds of regretful fretting. Don't let posed photos do this to you. In time you'll be able to look back and not feel pain, but in the early days, even years, they can be too much.

13. Change their name in your phone. You don't need to change it to something scathing (unless you want to). Simply having their name as the first initial can really help remove a big trigger from your life in the early days of separation.

14. Straight away treat any bank accounts as if you are going to have them audited. What I mean by this is act as if the divorce will go to court for financial resolution and you will have to provide six months of bank account statements, PayPal transactions etc. to be scrutinised. A good rule of thumb is don't have any payments for things on there that you wouldn't want a conservative aunt to see. In reality, the judge likely won't care if you spent £300 on sexy underwear, but it will make you feel a lot less stressed if you don't have these transactions appear in court documents. Cash is definitely king if you want to treat yourself.

Even in the most amicable split, exes can get very 'forgetful' and very secretive fast. Once the initial fear of being alone subsides, humans tend to try and protect their future. It's a useful survival instinct. What this can mean is that money gets moved, documents go missing and amnesia prevails. Get copies of anything you can.

Chapter 2

Looking After You

Bodily Punishment

Predictably the first thing I did once we agreed he was leaving was to buy a packet of cigarettes and a bottle of cheap whisky. I don't even drink whisky (well, I didn't). I felt like I needed to hurt myself, and the whisky really burnt as it went down. My sister saw my recycling bags one day and had a word about my alcohol intake. I decided to go cold turkey and it made me feel so much better. Getting divorced was hard enough without being hungover all the time. I am still trying to stop smoking, but I will get there. One thing at a time.' Terri, 39.

I can relate to the whisky. Having last drunk it as a teenager when it was pretty much the only spirit left at the student union bar by 1am, and thus a necessity purchase, suddenly I found myself drinking it neat, and in large measures. The burning felt like a good punishment for breaking up the family unit. Similarly, for many smoking is the punishment of choice. A habit often re-started after years of abstinence. Others turn to exercise and beat themselves up at the gym with gruelling workouts. I wish I was one of these people.

I'm not even sure you get to choose your method of punishment, more your punishment chooses you. This way of making yourself physically feel what is going on emotionally rarely lasts long so try not to worry if you find yourself behaving in a way that you usually wouldn't.

Bowels

On Boxing Day I went to collect the children from him at the agreed small country village (without any toilet facilities). I was very worried, I had spent Christmas day on the verge of combusting, separated from my girls for the first time on the big day, including one four year old who still believes Father Christmas only knows that she lives at home with mummy and was very concerned about not receiving any gifts. So emotions were high, anxiety was rearing its ugly head and, of course, I was prepared for the ex to be late (he was). I could feel my stomach unhappily churning. I knew what was coming, so I left the car and went to search. The church! The church would be open on Boxing Day. Off I went, tried the door and, hurrah, it was open. The relief I felt pushed my body into relaxing a little, meaning, well, the loo was now required urgently. But there was no loo. I frantically zig-zagged looking for a door. Nothing. A small kitchen, but not a loo in sight. I saw another door and, behind it, the bell-ringing area. There was only one thing for it; I grabbed an order of service, luckily printed on quite thick paper, laid it out under the ropes, squatted and pooed. Yes, I pooed on a festive order of service, carefully wrapped it, and deposited it in the bins outside the church. Oh the shame. To that church, I am sorry. To God, should he/she exist, I am sorry. It was the best I could do and I promise if there had been any other way, I would have taken it. Amy, 38.

I think the world is split into two types of people, those who vomit when distressed and those who crap themselves. You'll know which group you belong to from bitter experience, I know I do.

The brain and the gut are strongly linked so you may find during stressful separation and divorce times that your emotions rule your bottom or your throat. My advice is to plan ahead. Know where the loos are, have wet wipes, breath freshener, a small toothbrush and toothpaste, spare pants and trousers and tights. Tell the people closest to you if you're susceptible to your emotions going to your stomach. Just prepare and accept that things may be unpredictable for a bit, and it won't always be like this. Oh, and be careful of coffee. Coffee makes a dodgy stomach worse.

<u>Sliding Doors</u>

I regularly daydream that we never met and none of this happened. I feel so guilty but in these daydreams, I wish my children were unborn, like I could press a magic rewind button. I met him on a night out with friends in a bar we never usually went to. If only I hadn't gone out that night, if only we'd gone to our local. It's like being in that film Sliding Doors*, except I only get to see how the bad version of my life turned out. Josie, 41.*

When you're in the thick of it, you will fantasise about a life where none of this happened. Not just the divorce but the meeting, the kids, the whole relationship. It's okay. It's natural when you're in pain. In time you will find yourself able to look back at the relationship with more measured emotions. I think of it as grief for a life that could have been. I allowed myself to mourn a life I will never have, and you must too.

Instead of focusing on what your life might have been like if you hadn't met him, it can be useful to conjure a bit of nostalgia for simpler times. When I was wading through the divorce I often daydreamed about my childhood and how the biggest concern I had was if the Body Shop would have kiwi lip balm available on a Saturday. It was a comfort blanket when everything around me felt so very grown up and grave.

Divorce is traumatic, so dreaming of simpler times is a way to hug yourself a little. I wallowed in comforting memories so much I made a list of mine. They included: Eating mint choc chip ice cream at the park when it was snowing as a child. Walking to the shop at the end of the road with my pocket money to see if they had a copy of *Look-in*. Buying the Sunday papers on a late Saturday night out in London and reading them on the Tube home. Eating very cold sliced-up Mars Bars when watching a film from the video shop with my dad. Sunday lunch at my nanna's house where everything was served from stainless-steel serving platters and an electric knife was used to saw the joint of beef. The smell of boot polish on a Sunday night as my school shoes were polished for me. Choosing my penny sweets at the newsagents and being both happy and sad that the fish and chips didn't taste of fish and chips. Battered sausage and vinegar-soaked chips enjoyed in the back of my parents' car on a rainy day as the windows steamed up.

As you heal, the need for the memories and daydreams becomes less and less. Try making a list of simple, positive, pre-marriage memories to read through when you find yourself veering towards the *Sliding Doors* fantasy.

There's nothing you can do to change the decisions you made. Your past is fixed. The thing you *can* change is how you view your past. In darker times take control by assigning meaning to the experiences. I feel I have learnt a lot by reflecting on the unhappiness I experienced when I was married. In fact, I probably learnt less from the happy times than I did from the difficult moments. Funny, isn't it?

Learning to Say No

You know that saying 'if you want something doing give it to a busy person'? I feel like my face was printed next to that on a flyer and delivered to everyone I know. I am the fire officer at work, the first aid appointed person too. I'm a Cubs leader, the treasurer of the PTA, I knit hats for premature babies for the local hospital, I even volunteer at the park once a month to clear litter. I'm always running about from one thing to the next and barely have time to catch my breath. Did I mention I'm a single parent?

Yes, that too! I need to slow down, I know. I just hate letting people down. Christine, 28.

From a young age, we're fed the idea that being busy is good, being idle is bad. It's hard to shake this off as an adult. Of course, if you enjoy being incredibly busy and running from one activity to the next, fill your boots. My take on it, as a reformed Extremely Busy Woman, is that it's a diversion technique. A form of displacing any empty space in your brain so that you don't have to confront real emotions.

I have three children, and as I found myself making a wedding cake, for free, for an old work colleague I barely ever see (which I volunteered to do – no one held a gun to my head), I realised that by saying yes to others, I was saying no to me. And that 'me' included my kids too. I didn't have the time to play Batman with my three year old because I was too busy being a good friend/employee/volunteer. No more. I now say no regularly. At first it was very hard. I felt I had to justify declining to do something with a myriad of reasons. But I didn't. Now I just say no thanks as a complete sentence. If you can't bring yourself to do that, practise ways to decline with simple, glib reasons that don't leave wiggle room. Here are a few ideas:

'Thanks for the offer, but I don't have the time to do that unfortunately.'

'Thanks for thinking of me, but it's a no.'

'I'd love to, but I can't.'

'Thanks, but I'm going to have to pass on that.'

There are so many ways to say no without upsetting people, if that's your worry. Try Googling for more ideas.

<u>The Nob List</u>

My best friend took me on a really big night out not long after the split. I sat there, slurring how much I missed him, banging on about all his good points. She stopped me and reminded me of all the awful things he'd done in the decade we'd been together. I don't remember making a list of these but about a week later I found one on the notes in my phone called 'nob list'. I decided to add to it every time I remembered another idiot thing he'd done. Then whenever I was missing him and contemplating texting him, I re-read it. I would recommend making a Nob List to anyone! Romy, 32.

First off, disclaimer: anyone could have a Nob List made about them. We are all a nob at times. However, if you know you're prone to romanticising past love, having a Nob List about your ex is a really good idea, especially in the early days when yo-yo-ing between staying married and divorcing is more likely.

I made a list on my phone (admittedly it wasn't called The Nob List) in the early days of separation of all the reasons divorce was the right conclusion for my marriage. I referred to it regularly, adding to it often (oddly and perhaps as a download method) before I went to sleep at night. It really helped me to rationalise at a time when emotions were ruling everything.

One day I dropped my phone in the bath as I was scrolling. And the list died with the phone. Now it might sound a bit woo-woo, but it may have been the universe telling me to let it all go. I thought about writing a new list and realised I could barely remember half of them. It had served its purpose.

There are some pages in this book to start your own Nob List. Turn to page 201 to make a start.

Distraction

I felt like my mind was out of control in the early days. The only way I could cope was by distracting myself. I usually hate talk radio, but I got very into it. It was on all day, only turned off to sleep. Silence scared me as it meant having to face my feelings. Emily, 48.

My solace was in podcasts. I listened to entire back catalogues of true crime and business podcasts. I needed my brain to focus on anything other than my emotions. Next, audio books were my target. I invested in a subscription to Audible and chose my books based on the longest read times. I couldn't face listening to music, it was too evocative for me. Podcasts and audio books quietened the incessant internal chatter, but there came a point when I had to turn them off and face what was going on in my head. That was when the painful though healing work really started.

<u>Gut Instinct</u>

I helped him move out and sorted through all the cards I'd kept over the years – ones from me to him and him to me. I found a few from when we went through IVF that I'd sent to him, about me being difficult to live with and being sorry about my moods. I had this absolute gut instinct that he would use these cards against me. I removed them from his pile and kept them. It's amazing how right your instincts can be. Two years later, there we were in the family court with him suggesting I was too unstable to have the boys live with me. He had dug out old emails I had sent to him when extremely hormonal as his evidence. Ellie, 39.

When you are unhappy in a marriage, your instincts get dampened down somewhat. A survival technique if you will. I found once I was separated these instincts started to resurface and, at long last, I began to trust myself again. Listen to your gut, because if it tells you not to trust your ex, you're probably right not to. Err on the side of caution.

<u>Lightening the Domestic Load</u>

I am utterly shit at asking for or accepting help. It took having a near breakdown to realise I couldn't do this single parent thing alone. I needed help and I also needed to lower my standards a bit. I didn't need to have a picture-perfect home, nor did the kids need to eat home-cooked food every night. It was all too much. My mum intervened and basically insisted that I let her pick the kids up from school three afternoons a week. I found a cleaner to come in and do two hours a week of basic vacuuming and bathroom scrubbing. And I changed the kids to hot lunches which is such a game changer as now we have picnic-type teas in the week, which they help prep themselves, plus the lunchbox morning hell is over. Joy, 33.

Okay, this is a very practical bit of advice, but it's oh-so-important. Once you're parenting without another adult in the house, there are some things you will need to do to make your life easier.

1. Build your village

This might be your parents helping with the school run or a bit of babysitting, it might be agreeing with another parent to split the school pick-ups or Brownies drop-off and pick up between you. Maybe you'll holiday with your sister and her kids. Look to your allies and help each other out. Other single parents can be life-savers with this kind of reciprocal agreement. A warning though, don't take on helping another parent if they aren't willing to do the same. This is not the time to be a walkover.

2. Shortcuts

There's one adult now, so you have to think creatively with how to save time and energy. Perhaps you'll arrange the children's swimming lessons to be straight from school and have a car picnic on the way home; so dinner is taken care of for one night. Maybe you'll invest in non-iron school shirts. You might batch cook favourite meals and freeze them. You could have the children's spellings and reading books in the car for practising if you're early for school. You know your stress points, so think creatively and get ahead of yourself.

3. Lower standards

I hesitate to use this heading, but this is more about not holding yourself to extremely high and unattainable standards. So if the house is a bit messy, try to stress about it less. If the kids have freezer food more than they did, that's okay. If Fridays are for slobbing out on the sofa, watching a film together and ordering in pizza, so be it. We all have our own ideas of what is acceptable and what isn't.

4. Throw money at the problem

If funds allow you to, don't be shy about throwing money at problems. Outsourcing isn't just for the rich. It isn't about having a 'lady who does'. (Though it can be.) It can be as small as buying pre- chopped veggies or anti-bac wipes. Any little thing that helps is okay. For years I convinced myself I didn't deserve to have a cleaner, that I should and could do it myself. Post-divorce I have a cleaner and I love what she does for me. I justify the cost by reminding myself cleaning is something that I don't enjoy, it actually makes me irritable, and you know, we only get one life – for £30 a week I can avoid this irritation. You have permission to pay for other people to do things you don't want to. You do not have to justify doing this to anyone. It does not make you a princess to pay for someone to mow your lawn or clean your bathrooms. The martyr complex has no place in solo parenting.

In short, single parenting (or should it be double parenting?) is brutal at first. It feels enormous. You need your wits about you, so if that means letting someone else chop the butternut squash then so be it. Be kind to yourself, make your life easier.

Therapy

I went to therapy after a referral through my GP. I didn't expect much from it to be honest. Felt it would be a waste of time, some rubbish NHS CBT to tick a box that they'd tried to help me. I was wrong. It was amazing and I am now a huge advocate of therapy to the point where I tell anyone and everyone to go and get some. I completed my free 6-week course and then decided to invest in a weekly hour of therapy for myself. It's £45 a week that I can't really afford, so I have to go without a few other things like my takeaway coffees and ASOS habit. I don't see it as negotiable anymore; it keeps me sane and is an investment in me. I'd encourage anyone to try it out. I feel more 'me' than I ever have. Sara, 29.

I had an 8-week course of therapy through a charity at the peak of the legal quagmire of my divorce and I think it saved my life. I was so low, I didn't realise I could feel so desperate. I'd gotten to a point where I was catastrophising and the misery was spiralling. The therapy sessions were nothing short of brilliant. They made me reframe, look at how I could move forwards, and they also let me forgive myself for ending my marriage. I have been meaning to invest in a weekly session ever since they ended and just never got round to it. In fact, I am adding that to my list to sort out for today.

Still not convinced spending £40-ish quid a week is worth it? Try and see it like this; building a good relationship with yourself is THE most important thing you can do. It is the only relationship you are guaranteed will last a lifetime, so invest in it as you would a friendship. You likely wouldn't think anything of spending £40 on a meal out with a pal or a birthday present for your mum/sister, so why would you balk at spending that on an hour with a therapist? Many therapists offer reduced fees if you are on a low income or benefits too. And if talk therapy doesn't appeal to you explore alternatives such as EMDR (Eye Movement Desensitisation and Reprocessing) therapy or art therapy.

Work yourself out. Invest, be kind, don't hate on yourself. If you are full of self-loathing then you're in for a long and torturous journey. Oh, but also a word to the wise, don't tell your ex you're having therapy if you have children. Therapy can be weaponised in court.

Financial Injustice

I had to lie to keep the house. I told the mortgage lender that I didn't have any dependants. I know, it's awful, isn't it? But I didn't really see how else to keep it. I could afford the payments easily by myself but the mortgage lender said that with the kids living at the property I couldn't. Their words were 'a woman will always feed her kids before she pays her mortgage'. Anyway, what's done is done now. Zoya, 35.

There are inevitable living cost increases to being divorced. Having one adult's income under one roof instead of two, yet with the same rent/mortgage, bills etc., it's obvious. What may be less obvious are things like car insurance going up (yes this happened to me when removing my ex-husband from my car insurance policy, despite me having over 10 years no claims) and re-mortgaging being harder if you're a sole parent with dependants who live with you. Gather as much advice as possible, look into any tax credits you may be eligible for and don't forget you get a council tax reduction for being the sole adult in a house. If you have a spare room, you could also look into having a lodger, as some of this income is tax free. Check the government website for the latest figures.

Reinventing Yourself

I went a bit bonkers in the first few months after the split. I dyed my hair pink, I got a tattoo of a milk bottle on my thigh (I have no idea what this is meant to mean, so don't ask me!) and I had Botox and lip fillers. I looked a bit like a middle-aged Barbie. Nothing wrong with that, if that's your thing, but I realised quite quickly that I didn't like this new reinvention of myself. The pink hair grew out, the Botox and fillers have worn off, but the milk bottle remains. Thank God it's not anywhere it can be seen easily. Jerry, 48.

Okay, so frankly you should do what the hell you want. Your body, your face, your hair, your life. However, the self-imposed rule I made post separation, when I felt the need to change and reinvent myself was this: nothing permanent or semi-permanent. I didn't need any more trauma to deal with than I already had.

Yes, you want to wash that man right out of your hair with a new sharp, short haircut because he only liked your hair long, or you have a burning desire for a tattoo around your ankle or maybe a face full of filler. But please think about how you'll feel if you have One More Thing To Deal With. So, if you must have a tattoo, perhaps downgrade it to a piercing for now and reassess when the dust has settled. Same for anything that stays on or in your face for longer than a night. Save the big decisions like the tattoo or the pixie crop for when you are less emotionally fragile. Also, making a bad hair decision can take longer to grow out than some divorces. And you want to be fighting fit for when you get the decree absolute. That's the time to invest in a little Botox if you want to, resetting the clock to remove the time wasted on your ex.

Me? I lost my appetite for the first time in my life and lost quite a lot of weight. My girlfriends and I seem to be split into two camps when it comes to stress. We either stop eating or can't stop eating. I stopped eating and rather enjoyed the attention I got now that my spare tyre had disappeared. I had fun in a very dark time, trying on clothes in Primark that were designed with skinny teenagers in mind. But when I got happier, it all piled back on. If you find yourself over or undereating with stress, try to keep an eye on *what* you're actually eating. If it's very little, make sure it's delicious and nutritious. If it's lots, make sure it's delicious and nutritious. Simple really. Though of course easier said than done when you're upset and eating the kids Haribo stash for dinner.

Oddly, during my reinvention period I also started wearing metallic shoes and animal print. I have nothing against silver shoes or leopard print, but for some reason it became an obsession. I think it may have been a diversion from feeling all the feelings. Or perhaps galvanising some big cat energy. Who knows? Anyway, it's passed now.

Medication

After I received the first solicitor's letter that he was going to apply for the kids to live with him full time, I fell to pieces. I sat on the doorstep of my house and just felt numb. I thought about leaving and disappearing forever. I didn't even cry, but everything felt and looked a bit strange. Sounds were echoey, my vision was blurred. I felt like I was watching myself from above, it wasn't nice at all. I went up to bed and I didn't leave for four days apart from to use the toilet. I felt broken. After three days without any sleep, I was hallucinating. My brother came around and ended up taking me to the doctor. I was prescribed anti-depressants and sleeping pills. I didn't want to take them, but it was the right decision. I'm not on Sertraline anymore, but it was honestly the most amazing crutch at the time. The sleeping pills I only took for three nights, but they re-set my system. God, I was a mess, I'm so thankful my brother intervened. By the way, my ex didn't get the kids full-time. Caitlyn, 37.

If you feel unwell, see your doctor. Going through a divorce is extremely stressful. You are not weak for finding it hard. Seek some help if you need it. Start with your GP and go from there. And if you feel you aren't being listened to by your GP, request to see another one at your surgery. You have to be your own best advocate. You need to be firing on all cylinders when you're going through a divorce.

Divorce Porn

I became obsessed with a BBC programme called Doctor Foster. *I watched both series back-to-back. Then I watched them again. It's all about a woman whose husband had an affair and the fall-out of the divorce. I felt like the woman in it was my friend. She was going through the same shit I was. It's funny as now I don't feel the need to watch anything with divorce in, in fact I actively avoid it. But at the time I was kind of addicted. Lucy, 45.*

From separation through to quite recently, I was addicted to divorce porn. No, not Pornhub videos of divorcees getting it on, but any book, film, podcast or TV series with divorce as its central theme. It didn't need to be real-life stories, fiction would do. It seems I'm not alone in this divorce porn addiction. The interest spanned from divorce through to uplifting books about finding yourself and moving on.

This is not an exhaustive list, but I can personally recommend the following if you find yourself with a similar need:

Books: *Heartburn* by Nora Ephron; *Too Good To Leave, Too Bad To Stay* by Mira Kirshenbaum; *A Woman In Your Own Right* by Anne Dickson; *If I Could Tell You Just One Thing* by Richard Reed (this book is basically life advice from experts, a few bits of advice on relationships so not pure divorce porn); *Happily Ever...Fuck That* by Constance Hall; *Living With The Dominator* by Pat Craven; *The Paper Lovers* by Gerard

Woodward; *How To Do The Work* by Dr Nicole LePera; *Untamed* by Glennon Doyle; *Fleishman Is In Trouble* by Taffy Brodesser-Akner; *Women Who Love Too Much* by Robin Norwood; *Why Does He Do That?* by Lundy Bancroft.

Poetry: 'Courage' by Anne Sexton; 'Wild Geese' by Mary Oliver; 'Late Fragment' by Raymond Carver.

Films: *Marriage Story*; *Finding Your Feet*; *The Squid and the Whale*; *Kramer Vs Kramer*; *The Royal Tenenbaums*; *First Wives Club*; *The Girl on the Train*; *Heartburn.*

Podcasts: *The Divorce Club* by Samantha Baines; *Trashy Divorces.*

TV: *Doctor Foster; The Split*; *The Marvellous Mrs Maisel*; *Casual*; *Californication*; *Divorce*; *Girls.*

Social Media: (Not all of these accounts post solely about divorce, some have just been through it and are inspiring) The Holistic Psychologist; Caroline Strawson; The Divorce Coach; Helen Wears a Size 18; Tracey Stevens at The Healing Point; Alex Hollywood; Mel Knibb at Le Coin de Mel; Ashlie Sugar Rushed; Laura Anne Burdett; Jiggy at Jigna Made Up; Emma at 1 Five One; Stacey Duguid; Elena Lucie; Jen Brown at Meet You at the Barre.

Chapter 3

Family, Friends & Other People

Single Mum Friends

At first I carried on hanging out in the same group of mum friends. I didn't have much choice really, I wasn't exactly flush with offers of babysitting and I wasn't even sure how to make new friendships with women. Then, one day at a playgroup, I got chatting to Nush and we bonded. She was a single parent and always had been. Her little one's dad hadn't wanted to be involved, she actually called herself a double parent, not a single parent, because she was doing two jobs. She said she preferred it as there was no one to be disappointed with. I loved that. Well, it was an absolute Godsend; Nush introduced me to other single parents and we have ended up a really tight group. They give me such joy, because they get it. I am still mates with my old mum friends but I see them less. Janine, 36.

I think once you're a single parent you really do need the solidarity of knowing and spending time with other single parents with the same shared experience. There is no one else who will understand how it feels to look after your kids when you all have a tummy bug and there isn't another adult in the house to turn to. There's no one else who gets how it feels to go to Ikea and try to transport all your goods to the car whilst carrying a child and not being able to move the trolley to where you parked. And at weekends, your attached mum friends are usually busy with their husbands. That's okay, but you need to build yourself a support network. How? You have to be a bit gutsy. If you are in a queue and notice a mum who looks friendly and has a kid, strike up a conversation. People love to talk about their children, so ask them about them. Go to groups, get to the school drop-off a little early to chat to other mums, even ask your mates if they have any single parents in their group of friends.

Oh, and lastly, bite your tongue when your married friends tell you they know what it's like to be a single parent because their husband sometimes works away or goes on a lads' holiday every August. I don't think they say these things to be a dick, I think it's said with the best of intentions, to show solidarity. It's always met with an internal sigh of course. It's not the same. It's just not. Having another adult to speak to about the kids, who loves you and them, shares a home with you and has the same interest in their wellbeing is a hard thing to lose. Some women never even have it in the first place.

Not Keeping Up with the Joneses

My uni friends and I have had a yearly reunion in London pretty much since we hit 30. It's always been a lot of fun and involved a posh hotel, nice meals out and some kind of daytime activity like wine-tasting or making chocolates. I have amazing memories of these weekends. The year after I split from my ex there was no way I could spend over £300 on a weekend away. My budget just didn't stretch to it. I made up a load of excuses and ended up crying on the phone to one of my friends in the end. I was so ashamed. They wanted to group together and pay for my share, but I refused. I'm hoping I will be able to go in the future but, at the moment, I just can't. Chloe, 37.

There's a high probability your finances will become tighter after divorcing. You have to prioritise what you spend on and having had to navigate this, it can involve some difficult conversations. White lies can be your friend. For me the annual Christmas dinner out with the school mums I barely know had to go. I said I was already busy on the night they'd chosen. A group of people I don't know too well don't need to know the ins and outs of my finances. A cocktail-making class organised for a good friend's birthday was declined too. At the time I couldn't stretch to it, and, not wanting to embarrass the group of friends, I just said I had stopped drinking so felt it wasn't for me.

A single mum friend I know has stopped meeting her friends for dinner and instead pops by for a drink after they've finished, purely to reduce costs. She blames her babysitter, saying they can't come over any earlier. A simple, harmless white lie to save having to split a large bill that she can't afford. I applaud her. You don't have to spend lots to maintain your friendships. And you don't even have to tell them you can't afford what you once did if you don't want to.

Friends to Hold You Up

My best mate from primary school wasn't great when my ex-husband left me. She was really busy and didn't even ask me if I fancied a coffee, let alone a cocktail, until six months after he moved out. I can't pretend I wasn't hurt by this. I really thought after how long we'd known each other and how close we are, she'd be my rock. I'm not sure the friendship will ever recover, to be honest, but luckily I have other friends who have been amazing. Lyn, 44.

This seems to be quite common; that the oldest friends who you thought would be your emotional crutch, aren't always able to fulfil this role. The biggest surprise to me when I separated was that the women who held me up were not the ones I expected to. Some were quite recent friends. And, my goodness, they were amazing. I'm not sure where I would be now without them.

When I look at the gang of women who've wiped away my literal and metaphorical tears, they all have one thing in common. These women I adore have all experienced significant adversity, albeit perhaps not all in an immediately obvious way. There's the friend whose mother is toxic and difficult, there's the friend who's in recovery from cancer, there's the friend who lost her sister when she was a teenager, there's the friend who went back to uni when she was a grandmother. It seems that through their heartbreak and trials, they are the most real and true form of human beings. They're bloodily present in their relationships and I am so grateful to them. Pick your girl gang wisely.

Gossip Gatherers

If one more Facebook friend from high school asks me out for a drink I will scream. Not one of these people has shown any interest in me since we wore school uniform, now suddenly they want to hang out and catch up. And just when I've split up from my husband…what a coincidence! No thank you. Rosalind, 29.

Prepare yourself for 'expired' friends and acquaintances suddenly wanting to meet up. They're not your friend. If they were, you would see them in real life, not just an edited highlights reel of photos on social media. You don't owe anything to them and, frankly, if they're cheeky enough after not having seen you in the flesh for years, to suggest a coffee upon news of your separation, then be cheeky enough not to dignify them with a response.

I learnt the hard way about this. A friend I went to Brownies with in the 1980s who I haven't seen in person since 1989 wanted to visit me at my home for a cup of tea. I kid you not. I stupidly agreed and found she simply wanted to mine me for information. It was awkward and left me with an unpleasant feeling. The next time an old school friend suggested meeting up I politely declined saying I was too busy. They didn't ask again. Funny that.

You Will Bore Your Friends

I think I owe every single one of my girlfriends an apology and a big bunch of flowers. In the year after I left him I was SO boring. I couldn't talk about anything else and was a very selfish conversationalist. They were brilliant and deserve medals for putting up with me. Moira, 45.

There's a point in your divorce where you will notice some people may be a *little* fed up with talking about your woes. That's okay. It might be interesting and all-consuming to you, but it can be very boring to other people. If you notice the mums in the school playground turning their backs as you approach, you may have overdone it.

Having a group of friends to talk to is important, to spread the load. You can't push every one of your emotions onto one person. It's unfair. And though you are going through a tough time, you still need to be a friend back to your mates. It may not be intuitive to be caring towards others when you are licking your own wounds. It might mean you have to make a mental note to yourself to ask a question about their lives for every soliloquy about your pain that you deliver but do try to do it. Divorce can make you a selfish friend for a while.

Choosing Sides (Friends and How to Lose Them)

A couple we were friends with when we were married finally decided to tie the knot after over twenty years together. They're one of the nicest couples I know, and I dearly wanted to be at the wedding, but I couldn't face seeing my soon-to-be ex-husband. I emailed my friend and very politely enquired if he would be at the wedding, giving the excuse that we were deep in legal action and so I didn't think it was appropriate to socialise with him. I made it clear I wouldn't be upset if he was going and that I didn't expect the bride and groom to take sides. I received a reply within minutes and it made me cry. It simply said, 'when couples get divorced, you can't be friends with both of them, you have to choose a side, and we choose you.' Anna, 48.

It is very easy to lose friends when splitting up. I had to tentatively ask a friend something akin to the above at the peak of legal action. Her response was similar. It's hard to know what else to add, other than that she is right, but also that it works both ways. Don't blame some friends for moving to his side. Everything gets split in a divorce, including loyalties. Beware friends who are hellbent on staying pals with both of you. Don't trust them; their intentions may be well meaning but it's certain no actual good will come from it. See the bright side; that the friends you do have will be truly yours. The pool will be smaller, but that's okay.

<u>You're So Strong!</u>

I've lost count of the amount of times my friends and family have told me how strong I am. I'm not. I am falling apart inside, but I have to keep going, don't I? What's the alternative? Katherine, 36.

Gosh, how many times have I been told I am so strong? I don't know, over a hundred for sure. Shall I tell you what I think internally when people say this? I think that they have no idea. I didn't feel strong when I stood in court next to my ex-husband, just our barristers between us. I didn't feel strong when one of my children asked me why mummy and daddy split up. I didn't feel strong when my card was rejected in Lidl. I didn't feel strong when being interviewed by Cafcass. I didn't have a choice but to pretend to be strong, because the alternative was too scary to contemplate. If you don't feel strong, you're not alone. Fake it for now and just put one foot in front of the other. It DOES get better.

And the reason people say this? Filling silence? Trying to lift you up? Hoping that it's true? It can be very hard for friends to witness you fall to pieces. I think for some of my friends it was a method of praise and acknowledgement.

<u>The Popularity of Longevity</u>

I divorced my ex after three years. I knew I could tolerate the marriage and stick around for a lot longer, but I decided that I deserved to be happier than that. My family didn't agree so much. One day my mum was listening to me talk about the financial forms I was filling in and she lost it. Shouted at me that nobody was happy in their marriage but that they just got on with it and why did I think I was so different. She kept repeating that she had stuck at her marriage through thick and thin and was proud that it had lasted 43 years until my dad's death. I decided not to talk to her about it again. She might be proud of her long and deeply unhappy marriage. Me? I'm proud I called time on my short, unhappy one. Rosanna, 45.

As a society we applaud sticking power. We celebrate those who keep at endeavours no matter what the cost. The reason for this is anyone's guess. Does it show strength of character, a puritanical streak maybe? Dogged determination? This admiration could well be the reason many women stay in an unhappy marriage for a lot longer than is good for them. The conviction that staying shows fortitude and resilience. That the bad times will pass. That it's what the kids would want given a choice.

When your marriage ends you will have to cope with other people's strong belief that every year you manage to stay married is a reason to celebrate, and you will no longer be a part of this custom. Not unless you decide to marry again, and then you have to start at zero. You can't transfer the years you've accumulated like a pension plan.

Not being a part of these milestone anniversaries anymore, I look on now quizzically. Many of the people who post over-the-top anniversary declarations on social media have some of the unhappiest relationships I know. When you feel left out of the sticking power game, remind yourself that you didn't enter into the process of getting divorced lightly, whether you chose it or not. Divorce is not a whim. You did *everything* you could to save your marriage. If your family are critical of your divorce, firmly remind them that you would appreciate that they trust in your decision.

And remember, perhaps you won't be able to throw a ruby wedding anniversary party, but you will in the future be able to celebrate decades of genuine happiness, and, personally, I think that's worth more.

<u>Enough About You, What About Me?</u>

I bumped into another mum at the school gate and she asked me what was new. I realised she didn't know about the divorce so I told her. Said it was all fairly amicable and that we knew it was the right decision. She started to sodding cry! Proper big snotty tears. I didn't even know her very well. She went on to tell me that her parents had divorced when she was 11 and it was the worst thing that ever happened to her and had ruined her life. I didn't say much in the moment, but now I feel so pissed off that she did that. It was really selfish and not what I needed at the time. Sangita, 43.

This happens. People hear about your divorce and it triggers some long-buried emotions. They sob, they tell you it's the worst thing that ever happened to their sister/mother/them. They will tell you horror stories;

about suicide, homelessness and abducted children. A bit like those women who, when you tell them you're pregnant, go on to regale you with their horrific birth stories. Thanks so much, Jane/Lisa/Maggie, but I don't want to know the ins and outs of why you are now anally incontinent.

Remember, this isn't about you, this bonkers reaction, it's about them. You are poking the bear within them and awakening it. You can either zone it out and pretend to listen or ask the time, explain you are late and exit. I would advise the latter. You're not there to support people through their historical divorce trauma. Not unless you want to.

Once you tell people you're divorcing, be prepared to become a therapist. Yes, I kid you not. Just at the time when YOU need support most, others will use you as their counsel. They will invite themselves over for coffee/takeaway/dinner to tell you just how dreadful their marriage is and that they admire you. They will ask your opinion. They will ask you if they should do as you have. They are looking for permission. Want my advice? Don't say anything negative about the spouse as nine times out of ten they will stay with them. BUT, do give them permission to divorce if you want to. You can even repeat the phrase uttered to me some years ago. (See Permission to Divorce, page 15.)

<u>Other Women's Husbands</u>

The first time it happened was at a soft play party by the primary-coloured plastic ball pit. One of my daughters had been friends with Maisie since preschool and adored her. They were diving into the ball pit together as I looked on with Maisie's dad, who was married to Maisie's mum, one of my mates. He started to tell me how, despite it looking like he was very happy, his wife didn't understand him. Such a cliché! I tried to shut the conversation down but he would not be shut up. He ended up suggesting he come over one night to help me with the divorce paperwork over a bottle of wine and 'see what happens'. I was really surprised and declined politely. I was less surprised 18 months later when he was caught 'seeing what could happen' with Olivia's mum. He left a trail of dodgy texts found by his poor wife. I never told her about his suggestion to me, I didn't feel she needed more heartbreak piled on top of heartbreak. I wish I could say he was the only one of my friend's husbands to try it on, but he wasn't. And I'm not especially attractive, quite average really. I think it's the lure of the unknown, to be honest. That and boredom with the familiarity of their wives. Idiots. Sadie, 39.

It's such a cliché, isn't it? The poor lonely divorcee needing a service and looking to other women's husbands for that joy. Let me tell you something about being divorced; you will become very, very attractive to other women's husbands. Your best friend's husband. Maybe even your sister's spouse. Yes, really. One man (not known to me – a random Instagram follower) offered me his services despite his profile photo being one of his wedding day, with his WIFE in it.

Now, I can only guess why separated/divorced women are so attractive to many attached men. I wonder if we're viewed as safe as we're a known entity, whether these men feel the need to 'save' divorced women and see their penis as a method of comfort and saviour? Perhaps they think that they can gain one-upmanship on the ex-husband, by providing some much-needed fun where the previous man couldn't come up with the goods. Maybe it's pity? Who knows, in fact, who cares. I have long given up second-guessing motives for unsavoury behaviour.

What I do know is that these men are not your friend. They are trouble. They are to be avoided and ignored. You do not owe these men a reply if they email or message you with a proposition. You do not have to let them down gently if approached face to face. You are not a guardian of their relationship and do not need to alert their wife to their indiscretion. (Unless you want to, though be prepared to be vilified and treated as an evil temptress.) You ignore them. Or you say 'no'. No is a complete sentence. They do not have the right to make you feel uncomfortable.

What's worse than other women's husbands being so hellbent on offering you their 'help' is that a lot of their wives, often your friends, will be wise to this and see you as the enemy. You may find yourself suddenly dropped from social gatherings made up of couples or you may find your friends sticking to their husbands' sides when in conversation with you. Rise above it. This is a reflection on their marriage, not on your morals. They might not know that yet, but that's their journey, not yours.

<u>Divorce is Catching</u>

It started with Sally. She left Jon after years of his grumpiness. There was nothing wrong with Jon, but there was nothing right with him either. He was that classic middle-aged grumpy old man. Then I started to look at Andrew and see a lot of Jon's qualities in him. He was just a bit of a misery. Once I'd seen it, I couldn't unsee it. And Sally just got happier and happier the longer she was free of Jon. I think I caught divorce from Sally and I can't say I'm sorry I did. Geraldine, 54

I remember having a birthday party at the house for one of the children and noticing how the dad of their best friend was really quite off with me. He was polite but brusque, just not his usual self. I asked his wife, a good friend of mine, if I had done anything to upset him. She laughed and said 'we're having a few issues at the moment and he thinks you getting divorced and dating is giving me ideas'. What can I say? I think he may have been right. Divorce does seem to spread through friendship groups, like dominoes. Once one person admits the façade is just that, a cover up, others start to question their relationships. I think this is why when you divorce some friends will give you a wide berth. They don't want to invite the idea into their home. That's okay. You'll lose friends and make friends along the way.

Selective Memory Syndrome

My brother came with me to court, though wasn't a great help. I think he found it all a lot scarier and more stressful than he imagined and I ended up declining his offer to come to the final hearing. Less than a year later I was chatting with my family over a glass of wine and made reference to the court case. My brother actually said to me, 'Did you go to court?'. You could have struck me down! He was at court with me! I reminded him and he said, 'oh yes'. I think he must have blocked it out. Tracey, 34.

Turns out divorce is stressful for more than just the husband and wife. This selective memory syndrome crops up with family often. It's easy to be irritated by it; after all, it was you this happened to, not them. But remember that divorce shines a light on every relationship connected to the couple, and some people simply can't cope with it. They block it out to move on.

Comfort in Strangers

A lady on the check-out at Asda was so kind to me she made me cry. I was buying a Father's Day card from my little girl to give to my ex and she commented on how cute it was. I explained the situation and that he didn't do the same on Mother's Day so I wasn't sure why I was bothering. She looked me in the eye and said 'you're bothering because you are a brilliant mum' and then told me about her divorce and how much better things were six years on. She gave me hope when I was feeling awful. I'll never forget her. Leah, 37.

There is no solidarity like that of divorced women. You don't have to know the woman well, but the shared experience makes for such kindness it can be breath-taking. It reminds me a bit of the friendships forged in the loo with other women on boozy nights out in my youth. I've had more fun chatting to strangers after a wee, than with the man I was at the bar with.

There's an eagerness in finding other divorced women. A solidarity in the shared traumatic event. And not being close to them can be freeing. You can admit your darkest thoughts to someone you won't see again. Some of the messages I've received from women I don't know in real life included secrets they will take to their graves.

One of the most beautiful things ever said to me about my divorce was a comment left on my recipe blog by a woman called Adelaide. I have never met Adelaide. I don't know where she lives, her age or if she has children. All I know is that she is wise. I'll share what she wrote with you, as I found it so useful:

'Divorce is in many ways the opposite of marriage. It is never planned, not often celebrated, but, most importantly, unlike marriage, is almost always done for the right reasons. It's not about what you lose with divorce, it's about taking what marriage has given you and moving forward with them; being the wiser and stronger for it. So please don't feel any shame, disappointment, fear or loss of hope in accepting this new stage. Marriage can be a blessing, of course it can, but divorce is a gift of freedom. People don't see it because of the bad packaging that only generations of stigma and ignorance can bestow. It is not an admittance of failure, it is courage to say you deserve better'.

Being Out and Proud

My ex-husband had an affair with one of my good friends. I felt so ashamed. I didn't want to tell anyone what he'd done and so I kept not only his infidelity a secret, but the separation too. It took a Christmas of receiving joint cards for me to realise that enough was enough and that I needed to tell people. I wish I hadn't kept it a secret for so long, it delayed me getting over him. Gaynor, 40.

Only you will know when it's the right time to tell your inner circle and indeed people less close to you. But know this; you don't have to keep it a secret. And if he has behaved in a crappy way, you certainly don't have to keep his secrets for him. I'm not suggesting you rent a billboard to announce his infidelity or gambling habit, but pretending nothing has happened is delaying the inevitable and causing you more pain than you deserve by forcing you to cope alone. You don't deserve that.

Chapter 4

Legal

The Divorce Process

I wish there had been an easy ABC guide to getting divorced. I bought all the books but the language still felt so impenetrable. At the time I was very emotional and didn't have the band width to be learning anything new, and yet I had to. I know there are a lot of divorce coaches these days and if I had my time again I'd probably hire one. Mel, 51.

Okay, so the laws in England and Wales regarding divorce are pretty much universally acknowledged as out of date and punitive; as in they are designed to make you argue and fight, rather than happily move on. The best thing you can do, without a doubt, is get good legal advice early doors. It will save you a lot of money in the long run. If your ex is a narcissist, you will need to find a solicitor who understands the psychology of divorcing one as it IS different.

You can handle the divorce yourself and be a LIP (Litigant in Person) but it is stressful. Getting divorced is an emotional, psychological and financial shitstorm, but if you can soldier through a painful marriage, you can do it with a divorce. Honestly. And even if it feels like it's lasting forever, one day it will be over. I felt like my divorce was going to kill me at points. It didn't.

Anyway, broadly here is the process:

1. One person issues a divorce petition

This is called a D8 form and costs a minimum of £550 to issue (payable to the court), that is without legal fees from your solicitor if you choose to employ one to do this. Three copies will need to be sent to your local court, four if you are naming another person as having an affair with your ex. The person who issues the divorce petition is known as the petitioner. The person receiving the divorce petition is known as the respondent.

To file for divorce, you must have been married for over a year, your marriage must be recognised in the UK, and the UK must also be your permanent home or the permanent home of your ex. From an admin perspective, you need a copy of your marriage certificate (with a translation if it's not in English), your ex's full name and address and proof of your name change if you have changed it since getting married.

You have to give a reason for wanting to divorce too. You can't just say they're a dickhead. The current acceptable reasons are, I think, split into two camps, fault and no fault:

Fault reasons:

a) Adultery – that is your ex having sex with someone else. (You cannot state adultery as a reason if you are applying for the divorce and you are the one who has committed adultery – it can only be used as a reason if you are the person applying and are the one who has remained faithful). You can't use adultery as a reason if you carried on living with your ex for more than six months after you found out about the infidelity. It's also worth knowing that I have heard anecdotally that even when someone has been caught literally pants down, it's often rejected by the other side and, unless you have evidence (a child who resulted from the infidelity, photos etc.), it's hard to prove. It seems that even when a cheater is caught, they don't like it being called out. Oh, and if you name the person your ex had an affair with, a copy of the divorce petition will be sent to them too. I know for some people this is very important; they want the other woman (or man or non-binary person) to take responsibility for their actions. I personally think this is a bad idea and isn't going to make for a good co-parenting relationship in the future if your ex marries them, but to each their own.
b) Unreasonable behaviour – this is a great umbrella phrase for pretty much anything that's deemed behaviour that you cannot be expected to live with. For example, physical violence, verbal abuse such as threats or insults, alcohol issues, drug-taking, refusal to contribute to shared living expenses. I'm sure by the time you decide divorce is the right option for you, you'll have a list as long as your arm of unreasonable behaviour.

No fault reasons:

c) Desertion – if your ex has left you for at least two years before you apply. Pretty self-explanatory really.
d) You've been separated for at least two years – both of you need to agree you want to get a divorce and your ex will need to put that in writing. If you have had to live together during this period of separation (which is sadly really common given the legal process to

split assets can't be legally finalised until the divorce process is underway – chicken and egg, hey?) you'll need to show that you are not living as a married couple – i.e. you have separate areas to sleep in and you aren't eating together. Personally, I find this eating part really odd. If you are separated and amicably living under the same roof with kids, eating together seems sensible. Anyway, this is from the government website so I'm just the messenger.

e) You've been separated for at least five years – this option is for those poor buggers who have an ex who won't agree to a divorce. Yes, you have to wait FIVE years to apply for a divorce if your ex doesn't want to get divorced and you can't provide evidence of fault.

You don't have to approach divorce in a silo, you can do it together. I know of couples who grew apart and in order to get a 'quicky divorce' conjured up all manner of funny unreasonable behaviour to use as grounds. If your ex is reasonable (and you are too), you can approach the divorce together, including how you are going to handle the children splitting their time, and the division of assets.

Don't get yourself an online quicky divorce just to get things over and done with and fail to get the finances signed off by the court (either with a clean break or a consent order). If you simply get a divorce without the finances being signed off, you are not financially severed. Marriage is a contract, literally a financial contract. So, if they say 'don't worry I don't want the house, there's no equity in it anyway' and you agree, unless this is signed off in court in writing, it does not stand. There's no such thing as a gentleman's (woman's?) agreement. Even an agreement in writing between you is unlikely to be upheld in court. Your ex could boomerang back 10, 15, 20 years later and request their share of the equity in a property if you don't get it signed off by a judge. Imagine putting your heart and soul into your home and lovingly caring for it, only to have to sell it to pay off a financial settlement. Even if there are no assets to divide at the end of the marriage you still need this doing – why? Because you have no idea what the future holds and should you become extremely wealthy post-divorce, you really don't want your ex from yesteryear rearing their head and trying to get some of your money. This can happen and does happen. You must be very savvy and, sadly, assume the worst. Just because your ex is being lovely and generous now, this does not mean that once they meet a new partner, they will feel the same.

2. The court sends a copy of the divorce petition to your ex

This is where you start to see what your ex is made of. They need to reply to the petition with an acknowledgement of service form within eight days if you have used the reasons of adultery or two years of separation. This says that they have received the application with the reasons for the divorce, and whether they agree with the divorce or wish to contest it. The court will not chase your ex-partner if they don't complete this acknowledgement in the time period. And you'd be surprised how many exes claim they didn't receive the petition in the post. It seems court post has a special talent for getting lost.

If they are being a pain and failing to acknowledge the petition, you have some other options open to you:

a) Supply the court with evidence in the form of emails or texts between you and your ex demonstrating he has received the petition. Then you can make an application to the court for something called 'deemed service' so you can proceed without the formal return of the acknowledgement of service.
b) If your ex does not respond within 14 days and you believe they are still living at the address you had the petition sent to, you can instruct a court bailiff (if you are self-representing) or a process server (if you are using a solicitor), who will personally hand the divorce petition to your ex at either their home address or their work address. There's a cost attached to this.
c) If neither a nor b work, you can apply to the court for something called 'substituted or alternative service' where you are asking to try alternative means to notify your ex of your intention to divorce them. This might be by email, by a relative or even an advert in a paper you know your ex reads or is distributed where he lives. (You must keep copies of any attempt made to notify him.) There has been a recent case in the High Court where a judge approved service by social media. This may be the shape of things to come, but essentially the decision of what methods are acceptable is at the discretion of the judge.

d) Lastly you can apply for the court to allow you to dispense of service. You would need to provide evidence that you have tried extensive efforts to find your ex. So, in theory, it is possible for you to divorce your ex without them knowing it is happening.

If your ex has been playing silly buggers over the acknowledgment of service, and you have incurred costs to try and notify them, you can apply to the court to have these costs reimbursed. This is called seeking a costs order.

Once the court has the acknowledgment from your ex, they will send this to you so that you can go ahead and file for the decree nisi.

If your ex doesn't want to get divorced and defends the petition, you will have to go to court to discuss the case with a judge. You can still get a divorce if your ex defends it, it's just going to take more time, effort and money.

3. The petitioner applies for a decree nisi

Whoever filed for the divorce originally can now apply for the decree nisi with a statement in support of the divorce. A judge will then look at your explanation for wanting a divorce and (hopefully) state that the court cannot see a reason why you can't obtain one. You don't need to attend court for this. In fact, if you are not arguing over anything with your ex, it's possible to not have to attend court at all in order to get divorced.

If the grounds for divorce are accepted then your petition for divorce gets listed in the judge's list for procurement of a decree nisi. In other words, it's on their list to rubber stamp the first stage in the divorce. You will receive your decree nisi in the post. If your grounds for divorce are rejected by the judge, you may need to supply extra written explanations or attend the court to explain them in person to the judge.

4. The petitioner applies for a decree absolute

The decree absolute is the final stage in ending your marriage. To apply for this the petitioner must wait 43 days from the date given on the decree nisi (six weeks and one day). If the petitioner fails to do this, the respondent can do it instead, but they have to wait an extra three months. If you wait more than 12 months then the judge will likely want to see you in person to ask what's going on. The nisi, once you apply for it, takes about 10 days to come by post, or 24 hours if done online. Once you have the decree absolute, I'll warn you, it's pretty underwhelming. It's not a proper certificate, just a piece of paper. It feels a real let-down after all the hoops you've jumped through. Don't set fire to it or lose it; you'll need it if you want to marry again, or to prove you are divorced. Keep it safe!

So there you have it…it sounds like a really long process and it can be, but if you are able to agree on things, it's possible to keep it short. That doesn't mean that you should agree on matters just to speed the process up. Many's the woman who has regretted taking that approach. You need to decide what is important to you and what isn't. You won't win every battle, so if you can both compromise it'll be so much easier.

You may be asking at what point all the messy stuff about children and finances gets sorted… Ah well, read on.

Money, Money, Money

It was all going so well until we talked about our savings. He said that because I'd been at home with the kids and only worked part time in the last few years that they weren't anything to do with me, they all came from his hard work he said. At first I could see his point; he had worked very hard it was true. But we had agreed that I would give up my career to raise the children and the only way he could have children and work that hard was with me doing everything else. I went to see a solicitor and realised he was talking nonsense; that most assets are split 50/50 as a starting point, so it all got very messy and legal after that. I was awarded 65% of the assets whilst he kept his pension. He still won't talk to me and tells the children I am a thief and should be locked up. Nancy, 62.

You'll need to come to an agreement with your ex on how to split the assets, whether amicably together or through the courts letting a judge decide. This includes everything; pensions, property, savings, investments, valuable possessions.

Put simply, you'll either agree or disagree about how you split everything:

1. If You Agree or Almost Agree

If you are almost there, you can go to mediation together (either in the same room or in different rooms, called 'shuttle mediation') and let a third party help you come to an agreement. This is cheaper than court.

Once you have come to an agreement you need to draft a consent order (a legal document that confirms your agreement) and ask the court to approve it to make the agreement legally binding. If your agreement is not legally binding, a court cannot enforce it if there are any issues later. The consent order will detail how everything is being split and might also include maintenance payments or agreements for child maintenance payments. A solicitor can draft a consent order for you and will charge by the hour for this. The court fee is £50 for the consent order application and you'll need the original draft signed consent order, two photocopies and a completed statement of information (a form detailing all your financial information) plus one person needs to fill in a notice of an application for a financial order. If the judge thinks it's fair, there's usually no court hearing and it will be signed off and made legally binding. If a judge thinks it's dodgy, they may ask you to change it.

You can't apply for a consent order until you have started the divorce paperwork. Most solicitors will advise you not to apply for a decree absolute until the consent order is signed off by a judge. You can divide money and property after your divorce is finalised, but there's a possibility of paying tax on it.

2. If You Don't Agree

If you don't agree, this is where the court will decide how the assets will be split. It's also known as the 'contested' route or an 'ancillary relief order'.

Before you do this, you have to prove that you have tried to come to an agreement outside of the court process. This means attending a MIAM (Mediation Information Assessment Meeting) where you will discuss with a mediator if mediation would be suitable for you and your ex-partner to come to an agreement. You attend this alone with the mediator and it takes about 45 minutes. If there has been domestic abuse, for example, you will not have to try mediation, but you will still need to go to a MIAM and get the paperwork signed to say mediation is not suitable for you. Once you have this, you can proceed straight to court. You do have to pay for a MIAM (and any other mediation should you decide to try it).

Getting the court to decide how assets are split usually takes longer and is more expensive than agreeing between yourselves. Most people will hire legal representation too, which is costly. There are four stages to a contested route:

1. Exchange of Documents

Ahead of the hearing, you both produce a number of documents which are examined by the court. This includes the Form E, which details a breakdown of your assets and your debts and an estimate of your future living costs. It's supposed to be a legal document; shorthand for being the whole truth. Anecdotally, after speaking to many divorced people, this doesn't seem to always be the case. For many, the Form E is a great work of fiction.

To complete the Form E, you'll need to collect documents about your finances, for example:

- rental or mortgage agreements
- pension documents, including a CETV (Cash Equivalent Transfer Value – essentially what the pension is worth if it's cashed in)
- loan agreements, including cars
- proof of your salary income, for example your P60 or recent pay slips
- details of personal belongings worth more than £500, for example a car or house contents

The Form E is on the government website and is easy to download. If you are filling it in on a computer be careful to save it regularly. I recall mine resetting to blank on more than one occasion which was slightly soul-destroying.

2. First Directions Appointment (FDA)

The First Directions Appointment, also known as FDA or just First Appointment, is the first hearing in financial proceedings. It is generally used as a 'housekeeping' hearing, where the court sets the timetable and directions for resolving the issues between the parties. Each person will also submit a questionnaire in response to the other person's Form E, essentially a list of questions they want answered and information or documents they want the other side to produce. The other person is required to produce full and frank answers to each of these questions. This doesn't mean they will. More on this later.

During the first appointment, the court will examine each questionnaire and ensure each question is relevant and proportionate to the matters at hand. Some questions may be 'struck out' and not need to be answered. After that, each person will be given a few weeks to prepare answers to the questionnaire.

In order to split the assets of the marriage, the court needs to know what everything is worth. For cash and investments, this is straightforward. Where assets are harder to value, for example houses, companies or trusts, expert evidence may be required which the court will order to happen before the FDR. This will be done, generally, by both sides jointly instructing an independent expert. This expert will report to the court, rather than either side, and will use their professional expertise to ensure valuations are correct and useful to the court for the purpose of splitting the assets.

You will also have to submit a statement of issues; a document setting out the differences between your points of view. This allows the court to focus on the important issues and set the 'directions' (this is shorthand for things that need to happen) and timetable accordingly. The idea is that you agree the statement of issues together, but, in reality, this isn't always possible, so you may file two sets – one for each side.

The court will send you and your ex-partner details of when the first appointment will be. This is usually 12 to 14 weeks after you apply.

3. Financial Dispute Resolution (FDR – often referred to in conversation as 'fedrer' by legal folk) Appointment

This is a court hearing to help you agree without needing a final hearing. There may need to be more than one FDR appointment. It's a day of sitting in the court cafe, barristers going in and out of the court, talking to the judge, arguing and trying to come to an agreement that both of you can live with. Both sides' barristers will put forward their case and their proposals for settlement before the judge who will give an indication of what he or she would order if it came to a final hearing. There's a saying that a good day in court is one where both parties feel they could have done better.

Most people settle at this point in the court proceedings because their destiny is still in their hands; they are still able to agree or disagree or thrash something out. If you take it to the final hearing, your destiny is not in your hands. The judge will make the final order and you will have to live with it. You must take good legal advice and listen to what you are being told. Just because you think the system is wrong and that you should be entitled to more, doesn't mean you are. Listen and stay calm. Never lose your temper in the court. It won't put you in a good light in front of anyone. Also, you're showing your hand to the other side. Remain calm and have your best poker face on. Another reason people settle at the FDR is that most solicitors will advise that to go to a final hearing will roughly double your legal costs. This can focus a lot of people into trying their best to agree at the FDR stage.

An FDR hearing takes place on a 'without prejudice' basis, meaning the hearing in the court and all discussions that take place between the parties' legal representatives outside of the courtroom (including any offers made to settle) are kept private thereafter and cannot be referred to at any subsequent hearings, including if the case goes to a final hearing. Also, a final hearing judge cannot have been involved in the FDR.

4. Final Hearing

If you're not able to agree, this is when a judge will decide how you must separate your finances. Final hearings generally take place at court over several days (some over several weeks). Both sides will give evidence and be cross-examined by the barristers, while both your lawyers will make legal submissions on your behalf. At the end of the trial, the judge will make a judgment and set out an order transferring assets between the parties. The way the judge will come to this division will be based on lots of facts such as your:

- age
- ability to earn
- property and money
- living expenses
- standard of living
- financial needs and responsibilities
- role in looking after the family, for example if you were the main earner or caring for the family or home

- disability or health condition, if you have any

The judge will decide on the fairest way to divide the assets if there's enough to meet everyone's needs. They will make arrangements for any children first – especially their housing arrangements.

The reason for the divorce or dissolution is not taken into account, which I know when you feel like you have been treated very badly by your ex, feels wrong. But it's the law, so you have to suck it up.

The judge will usually try to arrange a 'clean break', so everything is shared out, and you no longer have any financial ties to one another. In cases where your ex has been extremely controlling in the past, having financial ties post-divorce can be just another method to exert control. Sometimes having ties to your ex is unavoidable though; the court sometimes tells the person with the higher income to make regular maintenance payments to help with the other person's living costs. This is called a 'maintenance order' and can be set for a limited time, or until one of you dies or marries again. The payment can also be changed if one of you loses your job or gets much-better paid work.

You do not usually have to pay Capital Gains Tax if you give, or otherwise 'dispose of', assets to your husband, wife or civil partner before you finalise the divorce. Assets can include shares, certain personal possessions and property. You usually do not have to pay tax if you transfer or sell your main home to your ex too.

Despite it sounding like the judge will decide what is right and fair for you, you're actually expected to negotiate and try to come to an agreement in the weeks leading up to the final hearing and even on the day itself. These negotiations can include provision for the children and are called 'offers', either 'open' or 'without prejudice'.

Without prejudice offers are never usually seen by the court. Open offers, on the other hand, are seen by the judge before they reach a decision. This means that the open offers help to define the bracket which the judge will think about when making an order on your case. Either side can make a settlement offer and under Part 36 of the Civil Procedure Rules, if the other side does not accept a settlement and then they don't achieve a better settlement at the final hearing, they can then be made to pay the legal fees of the side who originally made the offer. This can be a very powerful negotiation tool and has the effect of ensuring offers (and the consideration of them) are taken seriously, rather than a game of settling at the lowest possible amount. Normally you will be required by the court to make an open offer a few weeks before your final hearing. This will be a detailed proposal for settling your whole case. In reality these offers can be made right up to the day of the hearing though.

The length of a financial case depends on how many FDR appointments are needed and whether you need a final hearing or not. The courts are slammed and so there can be several months between the appointments. The court fee is £255 but the legal fees on top of this can make financial resolution cases extremely costly. There's a lot of admin in these cases, preparing the court bundle (the binder of documents submitted to the judge to explain the case) takes a considerable amount of time for example and this is charged for by the legal teams involved.

<u>Is it Better to Divorce or Be Divorced?</u>

I was unhappy in my marriage for many, many years and became a shadow of my former self. I always thought I should just soldier on, but when I finally cracked and decided it was over, I am so glad I divorced him rather than the other way around. He was still tardy in his responses but I honestly think he would have used it to exert further control if he had been the petitioner. It was the first step in getting back to being me. Helen, 38.

I think this is a question a lot of women wrestle with. Should they take control of the process and divorce their ex (be the 'petitioner' or 'applicant') or let their ex file for divorce, making them the 'respondent'.

My personal opinion is that whilst the petitioner (the one filing for divorce) does usually pay the court fees, it does leave you more in control of the divorce and the timelines. For example, you have the time to make sure the legal representation you have is a person or team you are absolutely happy with. If you are the respondent, you have 30 days to find a solicitor and file your response. Also, if at points you need to slow down or speed up the process, you are in control of when the nisi and absolute are applied for. If one of you is looking to remarry quickly (you'd be surprised!), this can offer you a bit of bargaining power. As the petitioner you also get the first argument in court, should you end up having to take the divorce to a hearing, you also get to choose which court to apply to (there are different waiting times for each court) and you get to choose the reason for the divorce.

Of the many women I have spoken to about their unhappy marriages, one of the main issues seems to have been feeling they have compromised themselves in order for the marriage to survive. If you are at the point where the marriage is terminal, taking back control and being the petitioner can feel really cathartic.

Legalese

The language used was like I was in another country. Half the time I didn't know what was going on and was too embarrassed to ask. So I sat there and got more and more confused and upset. Samira, 46.

Solicitors, barristers and judges have a habit of talking in 'legalese' – language littered with legal terms that sound like a foreign language to those of us not used to it. Don't be afraid to ask your legal representative if you don't understand something. And if you are representing yourself in court, you can ask for further explanation if you don't understand something. Be extremely polite, never interrupt and always say thank you. Oh and a warning, you will be called 'The Wife' in court proceedings, even if you are already divorced when you go to court for financial resolution. Many of us find this infuriating given you're in court to put an end to being called that.

Beware Agreeing Child Maintenance in Court

You couldn't make it up, he suddenly wanted the kids 50/50 having previously shown no interest in them whatsoever. My solicitor advised this was a tactic to ensure he didn't pay any child maintenance and to ringfence a larger proportion of the assets. Sure enough, once the case was over, he said that he couldn't have the kids half the time due to work commitments. Zoe, 40.

Kids are bargaining power in court, so some unscrupulous types do use them to make sure they get a bigger slice of the assets, then dump them afterwards. Definitely something to discuss with your legal representative if you suspect it.

One other thing, be careful using child maintenance payments as part of any financial settlement you agree in court. Once one year has passed, the paying parent (the 'non-resident' parent) can apply to the Child Maintenance Service for a re-evaluation. If you've taken less in assets for a higher monthly child maintenance payment, this is clearly unfair.

What's an Undertaking?

When we were married he had what one might call an 'interesting relationship' with alcohol. After we split his drinking got a lot worse and at one drop-off he was clearly drunk and had driven the children whilst over the limit. I stopped the girls from seeing him during this period. My solicitor suggested we ask for him to sign an undertaking not to consume alcohol in their presence or for 12 hours before seeing them, which he did sign. He's since been to AA and has pretty much turned his life around. I'm pleased for him. Ophelia, 42.

An undertaking is a signed promise by one person (you or your ex when related to financial settlement cases or children's proceedings) to the court to either do something, or not do something. They're a way of adding to a term in a court order which falls outside of the court's usual powers. They can be for reasons such as agreeing to do everything in your powers to release your ex from the joint mortgage by a certain date, paying a lump sum settlement in instalments, not leaving the children overnight without an adult present or not drinking alcohol/using drugs when the children are in your care.

They are legally binding and should only be signed if you are certain you are able to adhere to the terms of the undertaking. If you breach them, there are legal consequences which can include seizing assets, being held in contempt of court and even short terms of imprisonment.

An undertaking is a useful tool for when you are dealing with a slippery ex who is prone to interpreting orders to suit them. You know your ex best, so if you feel you need to really nail him down legally in terms of finances or the children, talk to your solicitor about undertakings and how one might help you.

Marry Again? Don't Make Me Laugh!

I don't see marriage as romantic anymore, I see it as a contract without proper terms and conditions, and frankly I would never sign a contract for my business without knowing the full consequences so I'm damned if I'll do that in my personal life. Aggie, 54.

I'll put this as simply as I can without sounding like a very wizened woman. Until pre-nups are legally binding and upheld in court in England, I will not marry again.

My boyfriend is keen for us to get married, I however am not. Once bitten. The way I view marriage now is as a financial contract. If I marry my boyfriend and we get divorced, my sons' inheritance will be at risk. I'm just not willing to take that gamble. The way I now view relationships is very different. Being married is no guarantee that the relationship will last. For me, the fact that my boyfriend and I are not married is more of a commitment. Every day we stay together because we choose to, not because we have made any declaration to anyone or because we have a legal agreement to be in a relationship. We want to be together.

He's still eager though. My last offer to him on the marriage front was that once he has the same to lose financially as me, then we can marry. I like to think of it as an incentive.

The Come Down

I thought I would feel so amazing once it was all over. I had planned a party in town with all my friends. But it didn't feel great at all, in fact I felt miserable for a while after. Jean, 47.

I can hand on heart say that leaving court at the end of a drawn-out case does not feel great. It isn't like the movies. You don't scream 'I'm free!' on the court steps. Well, I didn't and I don't know anyone else who did. I felt wretched, wrung-out and sad. I'd liken it to the end of exams. You've been looking forward to this moment for months, fantasied about the feeling of relief, and then, once you're there and it's all over, you feel a bit lost. I would advise having something low-key planned for the end of the case. I think it's good to mark it in some way, but be kind to yourself. You're likely not going to feel like having a party. Save that for a later date.

The Need for Overhaul

I work in local government at the council and so I expected things to be a bit archaic at the court, but it was another world. I felt like I'd entered some BBC 70s crime drama. Claire, 38.

Speak to any law student and they will tell you that it's well accepted within legal circles that the family courts are not fit for purpose. They are extremely busy, meaning cases can go on for months and indeed years. They are very old fashioned and rely on systems that were developed pre the internet age.

Things I found to be extremely annoying were my local court not taking debit cards for payments (cash only), having a very expensive photocopying service, counter staff being often brusque and a little rude, block listings (listing multiple hearings at 10am with the same judge, so that inevitably most of you are waiting around for hours and hours), there not being enough private rooms to prepare with your barrister, there being no penalties for not filing documents on time (despite this being possible), judges often not having properly read your case before a hearing, judges not understanding how to read company accounts… I'll stop, but of course there's way more.

Worst of all I think was the language used in solicitors' letters. Some of the letters and emails I received were unpleasant and upsetting. I had to keep remembering that these people were simply doing their job; it wasn't personal, though it felt like it.

A good way to approach the legal system is to think of it as your knackered old outdated conservative uncle, who hears selectively, forgets crucial information and wantonly favours those who present well over those who are good to the core.

<u>Form E</u>

Ugh, the worst thing about getting divorced is the Form E. It wasn't the actual filling in of it, it was gathering all the information. It was so depressing. And then getting his Form E was even more depressing, he'd detailed all the things he needed to live including a gardener, a cleaner, a clothing allowance of £300 a month… I could go on. It made me cry. He was forecasting some wonderful pampered future shopping in Waitrose and I was getting my card rejected in Home Bargains. Linda, 44.

What's the Form E, then? You can download the most up-to-date version from the government website to have a look. It's a lengthy form with every asset and debt listed as well as how much you need to live on at the moment and how much you expect to need in the future. The bit that takes the longest isn't filling in the form, it's collating all the information. We're talking all the paperwork for pensions, share certificates, bank accounts, credit cards, store cards, car loans, student loans, pay slips, mortgages, inheritance, expensive items you may own…the list goes on. It feels daunting for sure. My advice is to sit down with a trusted friend and tackle it together. It does need a bit of mental fortitude to deal with it, and, when you're in the throes of divorce, that can be lacking.

For the living costs, I was advised that women tend to downplay them, not wanting to look greedy. Men apparently usually do the opposite. So you need to futureproof your living costs. The children's pocket money might be £3 a week now, but it won't be in future. Consider everything; haircuts, driving lessons, mobile phones, birthday presents for parties attended, travelling to school or college, any clubs they may belong to, clothing, holidays, school uniform, sports kit, school trips including longer residentials. It all adds up. Don't worry if the total far outweighs your yearly income or what is available in the pot of money.

Oh, and when you get the Form E from your ex (you will have to exchange them at some point – agree a time and date for this if you suspect his legal team will try to look at your Form E before submitting theirs to you), definitely ask a friend to read through it with you. It makes for very emotional reading seeing what your ex-husband expects to need to spend on himself in the future. And it can also be upsetting when you see a copy of the court bundle which will include six months of all bank account statements. Seeing that your ex took his new partner to an expensive hotel in the same month he claimed not to have any funds to pay child maintenance may be deeply distressing to you.

Hidden Funds

He cheated on me throughout the marriage. I knew all along, and it hurt, of course, but I always knew it was booze related. He had a bad relationship with alcohol and seemed to become a different person when he drank. I could forgive him all the cheating. The thing that really broke my heart was that once we started the divorce process, he seemed to want to cut me and the kids off entirely. He wanted everything. The house, our rental properties, my savings (not much, admittedly), he started to pay himself minimum wage from his company so his child maintenance was almost nothing. He wanted receipts for anything I needed for the kids. I just couldn't believe my previously very generous husband who was always the one to get in the first round of drinks, wanted me and the kids to be homeless. I don't think I'll ever get over the meanness I witnessed. Estelle, 39.

I'm sorry to tell you that once solicitors are involved in a divorce it usually gets a bit fighty, especially over money. One solicitor I saw told me 'women fight over the children, men fight over the money, everything else is just narrative'.

Obviously this is a broad generalisation, but if you find yourself thinking that you don't care about the money side of things, unless you are independently very wealthy, you need to change that mindset. Because running a household alone, with kids to care for, is expensive. You need proper legal advice to make sure you don't get shafted.

The other thing I am sorry to tell you is that it's actually quite easy to hide money if your ex is that way inclined. Once you get into the financials of a divorce, you will have to be a sleuth I am afraid, and with that you have to prepare yourself for the fact that you might find out your ex has hidden considerable amounts of money from you. People can be really crap. I know, I know, anyway, how does one hide money? Let me count the ways (though this is not an exhaustive list)...

1. PayPal

Thought it was just for buying tat on eBay? Oh no, it's a really good way for some people to stash money instead of it sitting in a bank account. You need to request to see all PayPal transactions for the same period as their bank accounts.

2. Remortgaging

Do they own a property that they rent out? Or do you own properties together that you rent out? Get yourself onto the Land Registry website and pay for a search against the addresses. If there is a charge against the property at any point this is where a remortgage has happened. Yep, some people remove equity from their properties and hide that money, to make sure the pot of equity that's being divided is as small as possible.

3. Hidden accounts

Sometimes just asking if there are accounts in their name with Monzo,

Counting Up etc. (i.e. easy to open, online-only accounts) is enough to make them disclose. If you suspect a sum of money has gone missing, ask this question.

4. Companies House

If your ex is a company director then have a look on Companies House at their latest filed accounts – they are free and publicly available to view. If you don't understand how to read a balance sheet then set to work Googling. Just because your ex pays themself a low basic salary to avoid tax (as most company directors do), it does not mean they aren't taking payments elsewhere in dividends or other perks such as travel, mobile phones, cars etc. If there is only one employee of their company (them) do they suddenly have another one? Perhaps they're paying a family member or their new partner and they are giving the money back to your ex.

5. Pensions

Have a look at your ex's pension contributions. It's common to up these payments substantially to reduce monthly earnings. You must have your wits about you and get very good at playing a game of spot the difference.

One of the things that most shocked me about the professionals involved in the divorce process was how little of the above they seemed aware of. You need to learn how to explain financial data simply and without being patronising. If you feel there's considerable money being hidden, look at hiring a forensic accountant; speak to your solicitor about how to get this approved by the court so it's admissible evidence.

6. Putting assets in someone else's name

Suddenly a property is transferred to a new partner or parent or perhaps they close their company and all of a sudden their 89-year-old mother has taken inspiration from Dragon's Den and registered a business on Companies House with your ex as the sole employee. You have to try and put yourself in the shoes of a secretive, greedy person and consider what they might do.

It's no coincidence that the most amicable divorced couples I know are those who divorced without any assets to divide.

Victims of Abuse and the Courts

Thank God I spoke to my dentist about getting divorced. I'd told her in the past about how awful my ex had been, really abusive. She told me to look into Legal Aid and it turned out I did qualify for it. It was a lifesaver. I spoke to my solicitor about what had gone on and they arranged with the court for me to have a designated room next to the clerk's counter to wait in. He still sat outside it and stared at me but it was better than being in the same waiting room as him. Deborah, 39.

There is special provision made for victims of domestic abuse within the court system, but you may need to remind the court of this. Call in advance and ask what is available to you. Ask if you can have a separate waiting area as a minimum and think about how you are going to get to and from the court, especially as it may be dark when you leave.

You may qualify for Legal Aid in England and Wales if you have been the victim of domestic abuse/violence or if there has been child abduction. You can get a reduction in court fees in some instances too. Speak to your local Citizens' Advice; they can direct you to what's currently available.

McKenzie Friend

I didn't qualify for Legal Aid and I couldn't afford representation, so I took a McKenzie Friend into court with me. I found him though recommendation on a single mums' local parenting group. He was fantastic at explaining everything to me, helping me prepare court documents and just being a bit of a comfort during the court process. His rates were reasonable, too. Carly, 35.

I had never heard of a McKenzie Friend until I started the process of getting divorced. They are a person who assists a litigant in person (someone who is self-representing) in a court of law in England and Wales, Northern Ireland, the Republic of Ireland, New Zealand and Australia. They can be a literal friend, a family member, a volunteer you have found or in some cases they may charge for their services. Crucially, they are not a solicitor or barrister though they can perform some of the roles of a solicitor, such as preparing your court applications, statements, attending court with you (and going into the court room with you), negotiating with the other side outside the court room, and, on occasion, and with permission from the judge, speaking on your behalf.

Post-Separation Court Counselling

He asked me as part of the questionnaire he submitted about my Form E if I had cheated on him with my best friend, which was utterly irrelevant. My solicitor had said the best approach in my case with answering questions was to say we were willing to answer anything, mainly I think because my ex was being really evasive about answering questions and she felt that it was strategically better to be the 'open book' party. I ended up having to detail in a court document that I had cheated with my best friend and that I was in fact a lesbian. It felt so intrusive and unfair, but I think he really needed confirmation and daren't ask me face to face. Lydia, 41.

If communication had been a strong point between you and your ex, you probably wouldn't have ended up in court, so you may find the court process being used by one or both of you to make some peace with what happened between you. That may involve asking questions or finding out harsh truths about their spending habits and places they frequent.

The Form E and its supporting documents can make for emotional reading. You may see that your ex has been spending a lot of money socialising. Or that he's bought his new partner sexy underwear, or, as one woman told me, she discovered her ex was visiting gay steam rooms through his bank account statements.

Judges

My ex really messed up in court. He didn't seem to get that the judge didn't have to listen to his tirade of anger and that she could and did tell him to be quiet. I have never seen him so out of control. His face was bright red and he was tapping his foot under the table. I won't lie, I rather enjoyed seeing him put in his place. Martha, 51.

The clue is in the name. Judges, judge. They are human beings with their own personal experiences, politics, marital problems and athlete's foot. And with all the little fragments of experience that make them them, they come with a viewpoint before they hear your case. So, whilst I will not give you legal advice, (lack of qualifications and all that), I will say to remember that a judge will be judging you. And that does not start after they have heard all the evidence and your barrister (or 'counsel' as a barrister is often referred to in court) has spoken. Oh no, they judge you from before you enter the court room. They may (or may not) have read all of your file, they will be aware of your name. They will judge you for your name. They will judge you as you walk into the court. You will be judged on whether you stomp in with your head held high or if you skulk in, head bowed and avoiding eye contact. Think about how you conduct yourself. Think about what you are wearing (see page 76). As you sit in the court waiting area waiting to be called in, the court staff will be watching you. Don't think that by sitting and staring at your ex you are 'winning'. You're not. You're just popping a little tack of a nail into your coffin. Sit nicely, show respect, be pleasant and remember, EVERYTHING is a judgement once you're in the court system.

<u>What to Take to Court</u>

I had a court bag which I kept in the hallway. When the case was over, I took the bag to the charity shop, it had such negative connotations. In it were my stapler, highlighters, Post-it notes, pens, notebook, all my documents and spare clothes. And a portable phone battery with charger, that was a lifesaver. Anne, 39.

For me the court bag just grew and grew. Here's a list of what I kept in it:

- a black pen or 5 for taking notes in court
- a yellow non-descript notebook
- a bottle of water
- lots of change for vending machines and parking
- wet wipes
- tissues
- spare clothes including underwear, tights etc.
- a battery pack for my phone and a traditional plug-in charger
- my laptop and charger
- the massive amount of court documents

Don't take a huge entourage with you to court. As much as it can feel validating to take your new partner, his/her mum, your best mate, your mum, your dad, your big brother, your godmother etc., just don't. Take one person with you if you need moral support, but choose someone who will be calm, not whip you up, and who absorbs drama rather than creates it. You need the focus to be on the proceedings, not on anything else.

Solicitor, Barrister… What's the Difference?

I decided against using a solicitor and instead did all the admin work and emails myself. Not sure I would do it again, but you live and learn. I hired a barrister on direct access to keep the fees down. They were still £800 for a day in court but at least I wasn't paying £200 every time an email needed to be sent. Pat, 48.

The simplest way to explain the distinction is that solicitors will generally be working from an office and doing all the emailing, preparing of files and everyday legal work that needs to be done on your case. Some of them do also appear in court, this is called doing their own 'advocacy work'. Your solicitor will usually charge you in blocks of time for phone calls, emailing, preparing paperwork, writing letters, giving advice. (It's worth remembering that even if you hire a solicitor, you do not have to use them for every email/letter; you can save money by doing a lot of the communications yourself).

A barrister acts as your 'advocate' in court, hence it being called advocacy work. They are usually self-employed and work from a chambers (a rather grand word for an office) used by other barristers. They together pay for the chambers building and admin staff. They are hired by your solicitor to represent you in court and have a certain amount of time to read your files and prepare for how to represent you. It's quite normal to meet your barrister an hour before your court hearing. Barristers from the same chambers can and do go up against each other in court. I found this really shocking, but apparently it's normal. They are not colleagues in the way you might imagine, they are essentially just sharing office facilities.

If you prefer not to use a solicitor, (this is called being a 'litigant in person') but don't feel confident to represent yourself in court, you can hire a barrister yourself on 'direct access'. Not all barristers offer this service, so Google local chambers to you and have a look at who does. This means you will pay a fixed fee for the day they represent you without any hidden costs. Bear in mind that barristers' fees usually have VAT at 20% added to them, so factor that in. If you want to spend a large amount of time with your barrister to prepare for the case, you will need to pay for this separately and it's called a 'conference'.

I did all the solicitor's work myself in my divorce and I'll tell you now, it was extremely hard work and felt at times like an extra full-time job. I did it to save money. In hindsight, I wonder if it would have been better to have someone else lighten the load. At the time I simply didn't have the funds to 'put on account' (where you put an amount of money kind of behind the bar of the solicitor's firm, which they then use as and when required). What this meant though was that I received all emails and paperwork directly and it was emotionally distressing at times. I chose not to represent myself in court because the stakes felt too high, so I hired a barrister on direct access, though I know of many women who have represented themselves and who got results they were happy with. You know yourself and your situation best.

One thing worth knowing if you are representing yourself and preparing the paperwork 'bundle' that needs to be filed with the court is that many courts have a post box accessible from outside the court. You can use this to deposit copies of your bundle rather than queue up at their desk in office hours, pay for parking, lose time at work/caring for your children. I only found this out much later in the process and managed to make late-night dashes to the court to post my paperwork. Beware it will not be stamped as received until the next business day though, so you need to be more organised for this approach. Oh, and the other thing I did, after paying hundreds of pounds in printing costs at the now-defunct local Ryman's and on ink cartridges for my overworked home printer was to invest in an Epson eco printer where you fill up tanks rather than buy cartridges. I then bought cheap ink and injected it into the tanks with a syringe. Yes, I really did do THAT much printing.

Gender

I stupidly thought that a female judge would understand my situation and try to help me. I assumed not so much a sisterhood, but more a maternal understanding. But no, that has not been the case. I think I have experienced more kindness, understanding and sense from the male judge at the last hearing than I did from the female judge previously. Erica, 42.

When it comes to solicitors, barristers and judges, there seem to be a lot of preconceived ideas about the gender of the legal expert and how that might relate to you. When I called a barristers' chambers to hire representation through direct access (see page 70), one of the first things I was asked was if I wanted a male barrister. I think there's an assumption that a woman will prefer a man fighting her corner in court and a man will prefer a woman.

I actually went with female barristers, but I chose them based on who I thought had my back and who understood my situation. If you are dealing with a controlling ex who is trying to continue their emotional abuse for example, you must find a barrister and/or solicitor who understands this kind of behaviour and how best to deal with it in court. There are methods to best deal with narcissists in the family court; to let them essentially hang themselves.

What to Take to a Legal Meeting

The first solicitor I saw rolled his eyes at me when I started telling him about all the sex workers my ex had hired. I burst out crying which was embarrassing. He handed me a tissue and said he had heard it all, but that he would be the most expensive counsellor I'd ever hired if I used his shoulder to cry on. I didn't like him much and ended up using another firm, but he was right. His bedside manner was awful though. Bea, 44.

Time for some practicalities. If you're meeting a solicitor or barrister and paying handsomely for it (and even if you're not…hey, don't waste people's generosity if you happen to personally know a family solicitor willing to give out free advice) YOU MUST prepare in advance. You will need to know as much as you can before the meeting to make best use of it. Think of it in terms of preparing for an exam.

Take with you a list of all the assets (houses, investments, shares, cars, antiques, pensions, art, jewellery, savings, anything worth over £500 essentially), plus any debts you are aware of and issues around any children. You will need this list, a notebook, two pens (one might die on you) and two listening ears.

Don't mistake the time you sit with a legal advisor as some form of counselling. They have seen it all before, heard it all before. One barrister told me 'a client of mine was pistol whipped by her husband and this did not influence the judge's decision on finances' so prepare yourself for this to be more like a business meeting, rather than anything about feelings. Legal folk are bad behaviour weary. They're not there to tell you you're right, or that your ex is a bastard. That is what friends are for. Or if your friends are bored of your separation chat, it's what a counsellor is for. And they're a hell of a lot cheaper than solicitors.

A legal advisor is there to, yes, get the best for you, but not to discuss with you why the law is wrong. They know it's dreadful that a parent can walk away from a family and only contribute 15% of their income to the upkeep of their kids. They know that it bloody hurts when your ex proposes to someone else before you're even divorced. They know that you can't sleep and that you've thought about ending it all but, hey, you're the one holding the baby, so you won't. They know it all. Don't waste those precious, expensive minutes trying to gain sympathy.

Go in with a list of questions, take a level-headed friend if you can. Make notes. If you're looking for as simple a divorce as can be achieved, and believe this is possible with your ex, start the meeting by saying that your intention is to keep legal fees to a minimum and to try to remain as amicable as possible. Listen. Yes, listen to their advice. But also, if you don't like them, feel they don't understand your situation, or are concerned they won't operate in the way you want to divorce, you don't have to hire them. Oh, and also, when you make the appointment, check that they aren't something called 'conflicted'. What this means is that they have not already seen your ex or someone closely related to your ex. Nothing like getting all worked up for a meeting to find the solicitor you're seeing represented your ex's new girlfriend in her recent divorce. Yes, that has actually happened.

<u>Separated Dads' Forum</u>

I Googled a phrase he wrote in a particularly nasty email, to see if any other woman had written about divorcing a very angry man – I was looking for solidarity. I didn't find a blog post or article by a woman, but I did find almost the same exact rantings on a thread on a site called Separated Dads' Forum. Well down the rabbit hole I went and lost hours reading the vitriol on this site. It was eye-opening and actually really helpful when it came to navigating the divorce settlement with him.' Bee, 35.

I have a friend who reads *The Guardian* newspaper every single day despite being right of centre politically. Why? She says she likes to know what the other side is thinking. May I suggest if you have an ex who is difficult in any way, you check out the Separated Dads' Forum online. There are many other sites and support groups for dads. They are not by any means organisations set up with negative intentions, but they do attract some unpleasant characters (and some nice ones too). Do read with caution if you feel the need to research the other side though, as it can stir up emotion.

<u>Mediation</u>

I think I was quite lucky really. He was desperate to marry the woman he had the affair with and didn't want a long, protracted court case, so despite the fact he initially wanted me out on the street with nothing, he agreed to go to mediation and we kept it all out of court. It was faster, cheaper, arguably less stressful. I now thank the Lord that he had an affair and wanted to remarry, as I think if that had not been the case, he would have quite enjoyed a legal battle. He's a solicitor himself (commercial not family law). I felt the settlement was fair and whilst I think he would have preferred to have kept all of his pension, I think he's made his peace with it. We're five years on now and managed to go to our eldest's engagement party and have a civil conversation. He looked very tired, but then having a newborn when you're in your 60s is going to take its toll.' Ruth, 63.

If you are confident your ex is a reasonable human being and will want to avoid court then mediation is a cheaper, faster and less-combative option for coming to an agreement about finances and children. You do still pay for mediation (some mediators offer a sliding scale of costs based on income). The way it usually works is that you sit in a room with your ex and the mediator and agree on the subject to tackle at each meeting. (You can also sit in separate rooms – called 'shuttle mediation' but I personally would question how likely you are to come to an agreement in mediation if you are unable to sit in the same room). The mediator is not supposed to take sides. Anecdotally I know of a few women who have felt the mediator somewhat fell under the spell of their ex's charm but my own experience was that they keep a straight face, don't show favour and are there to help you come to an agreement you can both live with.

A mediator cannot give legal advice, that is not their role. They will listen to both points of view, try to dampen down any highly charged emotions and help you with practical steps to agree on things. Everything in mediation is confidential and is on a 'without prejudice' basis, meaning it can't be then used in court to aid negotiations. When it comes to anything regarding children, the mediator will be looking to ensure their needs are met and that anything agreed is in their best interests. If they're old enough and it's agreed, they may even speak to your children without you there. If you come to an agreement in mediation it isn't legally binding. The mediator will write a 'memorandum of understanding' detailing what you agreed with your ex and give you both a copy. You then have to pay for a solicitor to work it up into a 'consent order' which will need to be sent to the court and agreed by a judge.

There's also something called 'arbitration' which is essentially a private court hearing where you agree that an 'arbitrator' will make a judgement on your case and you will be bound by it. You should consult your solicitor to discuss if it's something that's suitable for your case, but, on the whole, it tends to only be used in family law where the parties have a certain degree of trust, don't need third parties to give evidence and where you are sure the other side aren't hiding assets. The same arbitrator will be used for every stage of the hearing and it can be held either face to face or just in writing. You would still need representation for arbitration, but it is a lot faster than going through the regular court process.

What's Court Like?

I think I've watched too much Ally McBeal. *I so thought it was going to be all grand and I would stand in a dock and it just wasn't like that. A small room, no wigs. I wish I'd known as I think it would have made me feel less sick on the day. Maggie, 43.*

The best thing you can do is Google the court where your hearing will be and see if they have an online video tour of the family court. If they don't then Google 'UK family court room' and you will be pleasantly underwhelmed to see that they tend to be quite small rooms, the same size as a corner shop in many instances, and the furniture is reminiscent of MFI. Whilst district judges do wear gowns, they do not wear wigs. It's most definitely not like TV dramas or films. (They usually feature criminal court anyway.) Be aware that family courts are often housed in the same building as criminal courts, so you may see judges milling about in more ornate wear for those criminal hearings.

If you have a smaller child arrangements matter that's being dealt with in the magistrates' court, the magistrates will likely be wearing smart but regular clothes (they are members of the public, after all) and there will also be a legal advisor there to help them with any law they need to bear in mind.

Once you have a court date, I would suggest you make a dummy run journey there on the same day of the week, aiming for the same time, to see how long it takes, where you can park, how long you can park for (there's rarely designated parking at the court, even for the barristers). Your barrister will likely want you there a good while before the time of the listing so factor that in.

What to Wear in Court

I feel like a veteran of the family courts, I've had to go so many times the security staff know me by name. If there's one thing I can give advice about it's what not to wear in court. For my first hearing I dressed up like an extra in the film Working Girl. *A suit, high heels, big hair, a full face of make-up, I don't know what I was thinking. I felt really silly when I stood in front of the judge. I was overdressed and looked like I cared more about my appearance than the hearing. I changed how I dressed for future hearings and was glad I did. I think my best advice would be to look as average and boring as possible. Tara, 32.*

I have been to court a fair few times and have learnt the hard way that how you present yourself makes a difference. Here are my dos and don'ts for dressing for court:

1. Don't wear black or you will be mistaken for a solicitor or barrister. Whilst this feels flattering, that is not who you are (well, unless you actually are one, but even so, you're at the court as a civilian for your hearing so don't dress for work) and it portrays you as a ball-breaker which isn't how you want to be seen.
2. Don't wear red. It's too reminiscent of the scarlet woman. Red draws attention to you, it makes the human heart beat faster. Red is not for court.
3. Don't wear anything revealing. Chest or legs.
4. Don't wear killer heels.
5. Don't take your most obviously expensive handbag or glasses or wear anything that is clearly a label.
6. Make up; either none or natural-looking. Avoid all nail varnish and anything but very tasteful and minimal jewellery. Even if your everyday look is quite quirky, this is not an everyday situation.

7. Don't arrive looking a mess in the hope it will make the judge think you are so poor you need 100% of the assets, they've seen it all before.
8. Do be tidy and clean with polished shoes.
9. Consider florals (I have always wanted to suggest people to 'consider florals' but, seriously, it's not a bad call).

Whatever you do, don't wear your favourite dress as it will forever remind you of court and you won't want to wear it again. I found supermarkets to be very useful for picking up a relatively inexpensive dress or trousers and shirt combo that looked smart and presentable without breaking the bank or looking too spendy. You can charity shop them afterwards. Or cut the fabric up and make a voodoo doll out of it of your ex.

In short, think of one of the most boring people you know, copy them, and you won't be far wrong. Or another way of putting it, imagine you are offered work experience as a doctor's receptionist and want to make a good impression. Nothing fussy, nothing silly, nothing sexy. Capable, grown up and serious. If you need glasses, wear them.

I am well aware this advice is deeply sexist, but, sadly, the courts are in the Dark Ages and a lot of judges are middle-aged men with outdated views of femininity. Don't be in a situation where you worry that how you presented yourself left a bad impression. Think of it like this; if you are someone who chooses to enter the legal profession and then chooses to judge others, you are probably reasonably conservative and you are used to having to toe the line in your own attire. People like others who reflect themselves back, so whilst it's not advisable to wear a gown, do think about what you are wearing.

Chapter 5

Children

What to Tell the Children

We didn't get many things right in our marriage, but we did get it right when we told the kids it was over. We made it completely and utterly clear that it wasn't their fault and that we had done everything we could to make it work. And we assured them that we both loved them more anything in the world. Rachel, 43.

Every child of divorce remembers the moment they were told their parents were separating. You need to do your best to get it right. Telling them in a calm, composed way, together (if possible) and being very clear that it's not their fault and that you both love them. Lots of women have told me their children wanted to understand the logistics; they needed to know where they would live, how often they would see each parent, when would one parent be moving out, would they still go to the same school etc. If you can discuss and agree some of the finer points so that your children feel they know a rough outline of the coming months, it will make them feel more secure.

Children feed and mirror our emotions, so even if the divorce is the last thing you want, try to hold it together until you are with an adult who can listen. And when you are alone with the children don't mistake them for your friend and support. They are hurting too. When you were married you would not discuss the issues in your relationship with your kids, so don't do it during or post the divorce. It makes them feel obliged to choose. That includes not hiding behind the 'they deserve an honest answer' excuse. They do, but an age-appropriate one. Not details and vitriol.

You Can be a Better Mother

I wasn't really there for my boys in the last year of the marriage. I was desperate to make it work and put my ex first in every way. It's when I realised I'd spent the family holiday budget for the year on taking him to watch the Grand Prix abroad that I thought it had to stop. You can't buy love. I couldn't make him love me, no matter how many ways I tried to. I am a good mum now and am proud of that, but I do feel bad for how little I prioritised them. Gayle, 40.

Here's a harsh truth to confess. I am a better mother since I divorced than I was when married. Now doesn't that go against the grain? The media will have us believe that single mothering is the reason for all of society's ills. It isn't. I think when I was married, I was just getting through the day sometimes. I am a better mother now. Kinder, calmer, more fun, more a yes person and less a no person. I am just more content, more authentically me, and with that comes better mothering. At times I remember some of my behaviour as a mother when I was married and I cringe; my focus was all too often on my marriage. I was also a hard person – closed off. In an effort to protect myself and keep a lid on how I felt, I capped off my emotions at 70%. There was a large part of me unavailable to anyone, even myself.

There's also a secondary element to my better mothering. I don't have as much disposable income, so I have had to be creative with our activities. Gone are the memberships to the zoo, the theme parks, the soft play…instead the garden is more used and the park too. Trips to the cinema are more likely to be film nights at home now. And with the reduction in outside attractions (distractions?) that used to entertain the kids, comes a newfound comfort in being silent and still with them. Just being. And I think it's a gift to help our children be content in the seemingly mundane moments of life, because chasing dopamine hits is exhausting and, ultimately, empty.

Love the Kids More than you Hate Him

I was so happy to be separated I was probably a bit mean to him after he left. He didn't see it coming and was very emotional. I felt free and quite energised by that. I was incredibly critical of his parenting and used to text him a lot with things I felt he shouldn't do, after the kids told me about his latest fuck-ups. It damaged our co-parenting relationship and has made him quite aggressive and defensive. I should have behaved better and been kinder to him. Pei, 39.

When you first leave an unhappy marriage, there can be an immense sense of euphoria. Anything is possible! The world is your oyster! Thank God that's over, now you don't have to walk on eggshells! Yes, but, also, if there are children involved, no. Try to ignore that initial release of leaving for now and remember that whilst your romantic relationship might be over, what you must now try and work towards is a good co-parenting relationship. You don't have the safe confines of a marriage anymore where you bluntly tell them you don't like the way they drive off without making sure the kids have their seatbelts on properly. It's the intimacy and security of marriage that allows you to be as frank as you wish. Strip that away and you have lost that privilege. Instead, you have (at best) a friendship, so try and act accordingly. If they do something you don't approve of or like with the kids then consider how you would approach the situation if it were another mum from the school. In short, you must try and look after your relationship with your ex *more* after you split than before. For your kids. And if that feels too hard and you find yourself about to explode at him, remember that you love your children more than you hate him. Count to ten.

Parenting Plans

A friend of mine suggested writing a parenting plan with my ex. We sat down together over a cup of tea and worked out all the nuts and bolts of the things we wanted to stay the same between our houses. It's been very useful when the children say the inevitable 'but dad lets me…' and we have even re-looked at it since he remarried. I think I am lucky though as he's a good guy, just not the right guy for me. Samantha, 35.

You can get parenting plan templates for free online. If you do have a positive relationship with your ex, they can be a really good way to iron out how you will approach parenting fundamentals. I would suggest you keep them broad and agree they are to be followed for the majority of the time, not used as a policing tool to reprimand each other with. Remember the plan will evolve as the children get older and gain more independence. They're certainly not for everyone (especially not advisable if your ex has been controlling or abusive) but useful for some.

Battles and How to Pick Them

I have had to learn to let go a bit and it's not been an easy ride. He approaches the children's care in a completely different way. They eat badly, they stay up late, he doesn't remind them to wash or brush their teeth. I get quite unstuck working out what needs a prod from me and what needs to be left. I mainly say nothing for fear of upsetting our somewhat fragile post-divorce relationship. Amara, 36.

It is painful to see your precious babies experience care which is alien to them and which you don't feel is in their best interests. The best way I have found is to try and split things into three camps and act accordingly.

First off, if it's abusive or dangerous, then you will need to find a way to intervene. You know your ex best and how to approach that. You can speak to the social services and/or the local police, all contact details will be online. Always document the issues and date them so you can refer to them if you need to later. Always, always photograph any evidence of abuse too.

The second camp I'd say is negligent care; not reminding the kids to clean their teeth, not making them do their homework, not getting them to school on time etc. This is the grey area where no outside authorities will be interested in him not parenting very well, but the effect on the kids is clear. This is where you come in. You're going to have to arm your children with the tools to negate this crappy parenting. So maybe it's that you make teeth cleaning at home into a memorable ritual of the morning and evening, so it sparks their memory when they're with him. Maybe you make it clear that whilst daddy doesn't make them do their homework, you do. Maybe you speak to the school about the day the homework is given/due in and make it clear to your kids they will be doing it at home with you, regardless of whether they complete it when with their dad. Maybe you have to buy your kids watches with alarms to set so they get up and out for school on time. Yes, it's a shame that some children have to grow up a bit sooner as a result of divorce, but it makes them resilient and independent, which are of course great life skills.

The third camp is the area where your ex just does things differently to you. Maybe he makes the children shower in the morning rather than before bedtime, perhaps he lets them spend longer watching TV than you would, or he doesn't read them a bedtime story. There will be differences in your approach and whilst it feels uncomfortable, you have to let him find his way. It will never be the same as how you would do it.

And then, if and when they meet someone new, there will be the changes in how this new partner will influence your ex's parenting. That can be harder to witness than the initial crap parenting. Hold your tongue and be careful not to say anything negative for the kids to feedback. Remember that children regularly misinterpret what adults say and add their own embellishments too. (Or outright lie – how many times have your children told you barefaced, often laughable lies?) If you are fed messages back such as 'daddy's girlfriend says you need to buy me new shoes because the old ones are too small', don't bite. This could have been a well-meaning 'wow your feet have really grown, I bet mummy will be taking you to have them measured soon'. Out of the mouths of babes.

Guilt

I have a lot of guilt about breaking up the family. The children had no idea how bad things were. It was a complete shock to them. They regularly say they just want us to be together again. I have lost a lot of sleep over it. Hayley, 27.

Argh! I wish I had a magic wand to remove guilt from mothers. It's worth remembering that guilt isn't the preserve of the divorced mother. Guilt permeates motherhood pretty much from the moment we find out we're pregnant, maybe even before. I recall the first guilt cloud descending when I was about 8 weeks' pregnant with my first son and realised that chocolate was high in caffeine and I'd been indulging a lot. He was about the size of a baked bean at this point. And the guilt hasn't stopped since. It certainly doesn't serve a positive purpose, but now I just make a nod to it and try to leave it at the door.

If you feel particular guilt for your part in ending your marriage, whether passive or active, have a think about all the things that go wrong in life, from minor to major. I don't want to create feelings of doom, but consider that they will perhaps fail exams, maybe have friends betray them, possibly break a bone and, at some point, they will all lose someone they love. Our children *will* experience adversity in their lives, and for some this will be their parents divorcing. We can't stop difficult and traumatic experiences from happening to our children but we can support them, listen to them, teach them the skills to help themselves cope (or find others to help them), and, of course, create boundaries to protect them from divorce-related hurt that happens to *us*, from being their concern.

Lastly, adversity shapes a person and softens them. It often makes them empathetic and kinder. So give yourself a break. You did everything you could to make your marriage work, be safe in that knowledge, and put the guilt down.

Drop-Offs and Pick-Ups

I read a book just after we split that said to always be the one to take the children to the other parent, rather than them pick up from your house. It's really worked for us. I take them to his place and drop them off, then he brings them back here. We always have a cup of tea too in front of them. It's not been easy but we have really made the effort to be pals. Phoebe, 29.

For many of us having a cup of tea with our ex at drop-off and pick-up is not going to happen. If you can do it, then give yourself a huge pat on the back. If you're in an unfortunate situation where your ex is being unpleasant and you don't want him to come to the house (I have heard many tales of men pushing their way in when dropping kids off), then agree to a neutral meeting point, halfway if possible. Do think about phone reception there (don't be bullied into agreeing to a location that's remote without reception), facilities such as loos or parking and also how public it is. If in doubt, go for a public and busy place. Not only because it reduces the possibility of unpleasant behaviour but also as it's a distraction for the children. If there's stuff going on wherever you do the handover, it takes the emphasis off the goodbyes, which for more sensitive kids can be hard.

Be prepared for your children to cry and say they don't want to go and see their dad. This is really common. And very hard. But usually fleeting. I found wearing sunglasses was very helpful in the early days. Seeing your children upset can trigger your own tears, which they really don't need to witness. I have always found being positive, talking about the fun things the children might do at their dad's and reiterating that you are excited for them works best. I also make it clear I have a lot of work to do whilst they are away. This admission that I am doing something boring whilst they are having fun seems to comfort them and allay any fear of missing out.

<u>Clothes</u>

He uses me like a free clothing shop. I send them off in clean outfits that fit and they return in dirty, too small clothes. It pisses me off so much I now have some cheap Primark tracksuit bottoms and T-shirts that are only for drop-off days. They never come back, but I see it as Crap Dad Tax and then wash whatever they come back in and donate it to charity. It's a cost I could do without but whenever I have mentioned it, he loses his temper and tells me that all of their clothes are his because he pays £78 a month in child maintenance. Awful, awful cheap man. One pair of shoes is over £40 let alone everything else that needs to be paid for. Belinda, 33.

One woman contacted me to tell me her ex regularly returned their toddler with only one shoe. Yes! One shoe. They claimed it was the child's fault for losing it, not theirs. Another told me her ex returned the children in out-of-season clothes. So the children would go in full winter clobber and come back in T-shirts and shorts. In January. This kind of extreme man-child parenting is infuriating, as is the using you as a clothes shop behaviour described by Belinda.

There are a few ways to approach the clothes and shoes issue. Some women prefer the suitcase method of dealing with clothing; basically that the non-resident parent doesn't keep any clothes at their house and you simply provide them in a suitcase at the drop-off. (This assumes you are the resident parent or have more than 50% care of the children.) I think this can be easier as the boundaries are clear, but can contribute to the children feeling that they are visitors in the non-resident parents' home. We did this to start with, but I came to hate seeing the boys' Trunkis in the hallway ready for them to leave. They stopped being a sign of an imminent package holiday and instead signified a traumatic event in their lives and a huge change in routine. They made the weekend changeovers feel laboured and more purposeful.

To move to keeping separate clothing at each home has clear cost implications though for the non-resident parent, and if your ex is disorganised or enjoys punishing you, can mean you are essentially providing extra clothes at your expense and being returned items that don't fit. It seems to get trickier as the children get older from what I am told. A five year old may not mind that their new T-shirt is at their dad's for the next 10 days, a 15 year old may care more when there's a party coming up that they'd planned on wearing it to. Oh, and if you have little ones, having two of the same teddy/blanket/comfort toy etc. is wise.

Whatever approach you take, be organised about how you send the children's things between houses, where the drop-offs are, who does them, the times…imagine if you were forced to live between two homes, had no say in the matter and sometimes didn't really know when you were going to be in either home or if you'd have your favourite belongings. It's hard for children living between two homes. When you're wrestling with your own hurt, it's easy to forget this.

When the Children are Away

I spent most of their young lives wishing for respite because he did so little and we didn't have any family nearby, and now I have what I wanted, it's so hard to fill the time. They're away every other weekend from Friday morning until Monday afternoon, and then every Wednesday night too. I don't feel ready for going out and meeting people, so I just stay in and knit, paint and use up their craft supplies. I'll get there. Faheema, 32.

I remember thinking that I was having to learn to let go of my children way before what felt natural; the late teens empty nest emotional rollercoaster was coming earlier, though fleetingly. In the early days of separation, they were away every weekend and it was very hard. I went out a lot, visited old friends all over the UK, I did masses of DIY, but I felt lost and a bit limbless. I found it hard to come to terms with my sons having experiences and memories in their formative years that I would not be privy to. Their private interior world of experience was developing faster than I had expected to contend with.

Going from a busy house with three boys under 10 to the silence of zero was like a thump in the chest. It hurt. But then it hurt less. And less. And in time I began to see it as recharge and admin time. I committed to being present for the children when they were there and, in the time they were not, I would get the boring stuff done; the cleaning, the food shopping, the repairing, the sorting of clothes that didn't fit them, the life admin of dentists and optician appointment booking. All the stuff that detracted from enjoying time with them. I batch-cooked too. A lot. The freezer was full of home-made ready meals. I had to focus everything on them and their needs during this downtime in the early days because I felt such guilt for having done this to them.

It's been four years now and I no longer feel guilty when they are away. I use the time wisely on things that I enjoy. Writing, reading, trying to perfect my sourdough bread, making candles, watching comedy, having late nights watching films and drinking wine, spending time as a couple with my boyfriend. I deserve to be happy and I deserve to enjoy the time when they are away. It is a gift to me, not a hardship. When the boys are here, I do a really good job. None of us should be afraid to say well done for the mothering we do, especially in the face of adversity like divorce.

If you find yourself dreading the time when the children are away, I'd suggest you make a plan in advance. Preparation will make it far less traumatic in those early months.

Here's a start:

1. If you're having intrusive thoughts and spiralling into angsty moments of wondering how your life has come to this, set a timer. You're allowed five minutes for the pity party, then do something else. You have to be your own best friend. Use distractions; audio books, podcasts, TV, music, whatever works for you.

2. Make plans to see friends in advance. Try to balance out married friends and single friends as well as varying the activities. It's easy to end up drinking too much in the early days of separation. Of course you may need a boozy night out or three to drown your sorrows, but alcohol is a depressant so tread carefully. Likewise hanging out solely with friends who are happy in their marriages can be distressing, mix it up if you can.

3. Make a list of those tasks you've put off and commit to three manageable ones each time the children are away. It might be finally getting the eBay box of unwanted stuff online. It might be filing all the bills into folders. It might be shopping around for cheaper insurance. It might be weeding the garden path. It might be changing the layout of your sitting room. Whatever the tasks are, get three things done. The sense of achievement is immense.

4. Plan something nice for when the children come home. Maybe research some well-reviewed family films for a popcorn and movie night. Maybe print off some biscuit recipes and dig out the cutters to make some treats. Maybe plan a geocaching day out. Whatever it is, make a plan and commit to doing it. I hate the phrase 'make memories', but you catch my drift.

5. Find one thing that is just for you and make a start on it. Extra points if it's something you can't do when children are in the house. It might be barre lessons online or yoga classes. It might be taking a Spanish class. It might be finally learning to use those old watercolours or going to a life drawing class. Or writing that book. Make a start.

Christmas

I always 'did' Christmas. It was completely my thing. I did Christmas Eve boxes and new PJs for the twins, I helped them leave out carrots, mince pies and a dram of whisky for Father Christmas and the reindeer. I nibbled at the end of the carrots and left them in a trail throughout the house. I helped them hang their stockings and tip-toed to their rooms and filled them with thoughtful little gifts chosen just for them. The first year after he left, he had the twins on Christmas Eve and I was a wreck. I felt that not only had the divorce ruined my life, but it had ruined theirs too. All I could imagine was their sad faces when they saw he hadn't done any of the usual traditions. I'm ashamed to say I emailed him a list of the traditions in November of that year, hoping he'd do them like I did. He didn't even respond. And, as predicted, he didn't make much of an effort and the twins were disappointed. Me? I was just utterly miserable and ate a ready meal alone, crying. The next year when I had the twins for Christmas, I tried to make it extra special, but I think made it even worse than when their dad made little effort. I spent so much on presents, they were still opening them the day after Boxing Day and they were overwhelmed. I think we've found our way now, but I will never forget how desolate I felt that first year. Amelia, 41.

Bloody hell. What a nightmare of a minefield. Brace yourself. Right, so first things first, Christmas is never going to be the same again once you separate/divorce. Make your peace with that now and accept it. And I know in most families Christmas is mum's domain, but it's likely it won't always be now. It hurts. A lot. You are allowed to find it painful but what you are not allowed to do is let your kids see that. Your job is to be upbeat and positive and happy and not make them feel guilty for having a good time on Christmas day when you're not there. This may involve lying a little.

You need to make new traditions. Everyone advises this, but rarely do people actually tell you what this means and how to execute it. So, here's an example. I have never done Christmas Eve boxes for the kids. I always thought they were a bit trashy and, frankly, wasteful, given the children were about to open a mountain of gifts less than 24 hours later. Now, I do them. Why? Because it's something they like, something that's new and different and something that they can now associate positively with 'Christmas after mum and dad split up'. Similarly, when I was married,

Christmas dinner was always a pork-based affair because that's what my ex-husband liked. I have nothing against pork but now it's not what we have for Christmas dinner. It's turkey all the way now. I needed to change this to make it my own.

Now you might want to do something else – maybe taking them to the panto? Maybe the more altruistic amongst you will take gifts to the local hospital or women's refuge with the kids? Maybe you'll bake a last-minute Christmas cake together? Maybe you'll leave out gin and Matchmakers for Santa rather than whiskey and mince pies. Maybe you'll start doing Elf on the bloody Shelf. Whatever it is, find something that's new and liked. Then do it every single year.

On to whether you are alternating Christmas. If your ex is happy to let you do Christmas Eve and Day with the kids, then thank your lucky stars and keep him onside. This is golden stuff. Most families either split the big day in half or take it in turns. Who knows what's best for the kids, but I am of the opinion that having chunks of time to play with new toys and see family is better than splitting days in half. To each their own.

<u>Mother's Day</u>

The first Mother's Day after we split, he had the girls for the day. There was no card, no gift, not even a phone call. Usually I don't even care about Mother's Day that much, but it really did smart. Especially when I made an effort the previous Father's Day, despite us having already split then. I ended up drinking way too much gin and cried myself to sleep. When they got home, I found out he'd helped them make cards for their step mum but not me. My heart broke a bit more that day. Lydia, 30.

You are absolutely right to think that a good dad should help their kids make cards for their mum for Mother's Day and pay for carefully chosen, thoughtful gifts. You are right that a good mum does the same back for their children's dad on Father's Day. Unfortunately some men (and women) weaponise their children to upset the other parent. And some parents are just a bit rubbish and forget celebrations.

If you celebrate Mother's Day (and I do, because I think it's really important for my sons to celebrate the main woman in their lives), you need to take control of it rather than allow your ex to influence your mood. If you are amicable with your ex agree that you will each have the children on Mother's/Father's Day, regardless of whose weekend it is. If you are not friendly, then have this written into a Child Arrangements Order. Then, if your children are young, ask a friend to take them shopping with some of your money to help them buy you a gift. If they're older and responsible, let them loose on your Amazon account with a budget. If they're even older send them off to the shops with a list of things you like. You do deserve to be celebrated so make sure it happens.

Should you carry on helping them make cards and buy gifts for your ex for Father's Day, even if he doesn't return the favour? I think so. I don't let anyone influence me to lower my standards and in my case, the best thing for the children is to help them celebrate their dad. I always think of the Michelle Obama quote in situations where you feel there's a disparity at play - 'when they go low, we go high.'

Travelling Abroad

My 13 year old got pulled aside at the airport and asked who I was. It was very embarrassing and he ended up crying on the plane. I now travel with a letter from the children's dad saying he gives permission for them to leave the UK with me and volunteer it before the children are asked. Fay, 41.

If you have a different surname post-divorce to your children, it's worth getting a letter signed by your ex stating his permission for you to travel with them. If you have a Child Arrangements Order then take a copy of this too. It feels horrible if you're asked, but try to see it as your small part to play in a system designed to stop kids from being abducted.

Kids are Selfish

My son had to write about his summer holiday in his first week back at school. He got a gold star for it and won 'writer of the week' and was so proud to show me. I felt so downhearted that everything he'd written about were things he'd done with his dad. There was a full re-telling of a weekend at Legoland in the Legoland hotel, as well as their holiday to Florida, his dinners out at Pizza Hut, his new PS5, his trip to the zoo and private tour of the meerkat enclosure…it was a long list of amazing day trips and holidays. Nothing about our park trips, film nights at home, visiting his cousins and staying up late to play Twister, Nerf gun battles in the garden with me and his uncle etc. I have to admit I was a bit disappointed in my boy, that he only mentioned the impressive stuff. I felt like all my effort was pointless. I just can't compete financially with my ex and my son preferring time with him bloody hurts. Victoria, 29.

The survival of the human race depends upon children being selfish. They have to put themselves first in order to reach an age at which they can then have children of their own. Positioning this selfishness in this evolutionary-human-race-survivalist fashion will make it more palatable when your son or daughter announces they have decided to spend the whole summer with dad because he will let them do as they like. It makes their waxing lyrical about the very expensive iPad they have at your ex's house easier to understand. It's a spoonful of sugar to help with their preference for a Disney holiday over something a little more, ahem, affordable.

Raising kids is a long game. And raising kids after divorcing/separating is an even longer game. It's a doctorate in biting your tongue and biding your time. When they are 30, remember, they won't be telling you how amazing their dad is because he let them get pissed at the park when they were 12. They'll see it all for what it is. I know that doesn't make it easier, but try and play a long and, more importantly, calm game.

Parent Pleasing

We ended up having to go to a family mediator because we each thought our daughter wanted to live with us and couldn't agree a way forward. I didn't believe our little girl wanted to live with him. I thought it was just him being his usual self and trying to hurt me by manipulating the situation so that she lived with him most of the time, knowing it would break my heart. The mediator said that she did want to live with him. And also with me. In fact, she wanted us to get back together! We ended up settling on a 50/50 arrangement to be reviewed in two years. I can't say I'm happy with it, but I've had to accept that she really does want to spend a lot of time with him at the moment. I'm so worried that when he gets a girlfriend he won't be as bothered with her, but I have had to let go a bit. It is very painful, I won't lie. Greta, 26.

Here's a hard truth. What your children say to you, could just be what they think you want to hear. Parent pleasing. They are way more switched on than any of us give them credit for. They are also deeply conflicted when the two people they love most in the world no longer love each other. So if dad wants them to come and live with him and they are aware of this, they will likely tell him that they want to. At the same time (and even on the same day) they could be telling you they absolutely want to stay living with you and just want to visit dad. Both are true. Which sounds tautological, but it isn't. They have their own separate relationships with each of you and so when they are with you, they are one version of themselves. Likewise, with your ex they are another. It's tough for them. They just want everyone to get along and be happy. If you can reach major decisions such as living arrangements between you, you can help your kids a lot. Of course, take into account their wishes, but do this without giving them the responsibility of the decision; too much choice is paralysing. And asking kids to make grown-up decisions can be too much for them. They're kids. When you were together you didn't ask their opinion about where they lived, so tread carefully. Divorce is often blamed with making kids grow up too fast, but I think really it's that parents often involve them in very adult decisions that arise through divorce.

<u>All of the Presents, None of the Time</u>

My daughter has a lot of requests for toys and clothes. She's that generation of YouTube watchers, spends a lot of time binging on unboxing videos and coveting new detritus. Her dad is more than happy to indulge her love of shopping and I have felt a bit frustrated at times, as I am on a really reduced income due to needing to work school-friendly hours. Anyway, one thing I have noticed is that she never talks about playing with any of the new toys or doing dressing up shows with her new clothes. I think I have slowly (and somewhat late) come to the realisation that the dopamine hit my daughter gets from these new shiny things doesn't last long and actually all she wants is her dad's time to play with her, which he doesn't seem to do. The one thing I do have is time, so I'm focusing on that. Emma, 40.

Kids are self-absorbed little buggers. That's not a slur. It's a fact. And it's a handy thing because they need to be in order to develop and grow. They are literally the future, and in order to secure the future of the human race, kids have to put themselves first. (More on this in Kids are Selfish, page 91). Now why is this relevant? Because we as their mothers can so easily feel very much discarded in their growing pains. And none more so than when they are the kids of an acrimonious divorce.

A lot of parents play the pick-me game with material goods; some intentionally and some because they are trying to use gifts as a sticking plaster. And kids being kids can be swayed by it. But remember this; that, really, all children want is your time. The games console is pointless if they don't have a parent to teach to play it, the football strip not as adored if there's no one there watching the game. The children's make-up kit isn't any fun unless they have a willing ~~victim~~ visitor at their salon. Give them your time and your attention. Be present. Put your phone down. Stop scrolling. Put as much time into your kids as you do social media/reading/cleaning/watching TV. Toddlers in particular are fantastic reminders of this; they are little truth bombs. If they regularly try to reunite you with your phone, you are spending too much time on it. Again, be present.

Don't Worry, One Day They'll Realise

My ex isn't a good guy. In fact, he's the definition of a deadbeat dad! He promises the kids all sorts and doesn't deliver. He's forgotten to collect them for his weekend more than once. He even sent one of the kids to school in his sister's pants, which caused a lot of teasing when he got changed for PE. They still idolise him though – he really can't put a step wrong in their eyes. I've lost count of the times my friends and family have said 'don't worry, one day they'll realise what he's like'. They don't get it. I don't want my precious beautiful children to ever realise what he's like. I want him to step up and be a better parent. But that's the one thing he wouldn't do when we were married so he certainly won't do it now. Nadia, 31.

It's maddening when friends try to make it all better with this comment. Put yourself in their position though, what are they supposed to say? And in some ways, it *is* a small bit of solace when you're in a sea of chaos with a difficult and incompetent ex, that one day, when your children are adults they'll see your ex for who they are.

As an adult we can accept our parent's failings and still love them. There's an acceptance with age of others older than us being fallible. Which translates as your children may well be able to forgive some of the shitty parenting they experienced from your ex. Or they may vote with their feet and choose not to forgive, and you won't be able to do anything about this. A huge part of separation and divorce is relinquishing control.

Child Maintenance

Initially he gave me cash whenever he picked the boys up and it was all friendly and fine. If anything, he was generous. Then I met someone else and he stopped paying. I had to go through the Child Maintenance Service. I have never felt so ashamed. I now get a regular monthly payment. It's not much, but it's better than nothing. I never thought he would be like this, he was always a very generous man. Gabbi, 31.

Children cost money, this won't be news to you. Once you divorce the costs of raising your children still need to be met, by both parents. It is a legal responsibility in the UK to contribute to the raising of your children, regardless of whether you see them or not.

The usual way it works is that the non-resident parent (parent the kids do not live with the majority of the time) pays the resident parent (parent the kids live with the majority of the time) on a monthly basis. Given around 90% of resident parents in the UK are women, this means your ex-husband will need to pay you towards the upkeep of the kids. A private agreement on how much should be paid can and does work really well for lots of people. For some it becomes a method of control; the ex requests receipts are provided and feels he essentially 'employs' the mother so can treat her accordingly, the money becomes something he will withdraw if and when he feels it's not deserved. Sometimes if the mother suggests she goes through the Child Maintenance Service (CMS) then the ex threatens that he will make himself jobless in order to avoid paying her.

You know your ex best. If he is behaving like this and making threats, is he likely to go through with them? One woman who spoke to me is registered as disabled and relies heavily on her ex-husband's sporadic payments, but she daren't apply through the CMS for fear she will get almost nothing as he mainly works cash in hand and CMS payments are based on declared income.

If you can't come to a private agreement then you can apply through the CMS for child maintenance. You don't need permission from the other parent to do this. You don't even have to tell them. There is an online calculator on the government website to give you an idea of what you will get. Calculations are based on lots of things; declared income to HMRC, other children of his he is supporting, any children who may live with him (even if they are not his, for example if his new partner has children and they all live together), how many nights a year the children stay with him and he can even have travel costs deducted if he has to spend over £10 per week to see the children. As a starting point to give you a rough idea, where the children spend 100% of their time with you, for one child your ex will pay 12% of their gross income, for two children 16% and for three or more, 19%. It's payable until the child finishes their secondary education up to the age of 20. Gross income is the amount your ex is paid before any tax or national insurance payments are removed, but after any pension payments are taken. If your ex has a new wife or partner then their income will not be taken into account in terms of calculations. Child maintenance is rarely paid where there is 50/50 shared care. If your ex has shown little interest in spending 50% of his year with the children but suddenly does once you open a case with the CMS, be wary. Does he genuinely want to spend meaningful time with the children or is it to minimise payments?

Keep in mind if your ex is self-employed, his payments will be based on his last tax return submitted which is not going to be this year. If your ex lives outside of the UK, if your child needs extra funds due to a disability, if your child needs extra funds for their education or if your ex earns more than £3000 a week/156k a year and you want to top up your maintenance from the CMS (and why shouldn't you claim this for the benefit of your children?) you will have to go to court to arrange maintenance. The CMS doesn't take these extra costs into account in its calculations. For high earners, for example, the CMS only calculates the percentage payable from a maximum of 156k per year. Now I know what some of you are thinking...who needs more than 12% of 156k to raise one child? If you believe your child is worth literal crumbs of what you ex earns then I would suggest you look at why you are conditioned to believe that.

If you have a private agreement for child maintenance payments and your ex suddenly stops or reduces payments, be aware you can only get backdated payments enforced by the CMS from the date you register the case, which is very easy to do. It costs £20 to open a case, though this is waived if there has been domestic abuse.

If your ex is a company director and pays himself a small basic salary to avoid tax (perfectly legal), then you may be shocked when you receive a letter from the CMS with a paltry sum as the monthly payments. Especially if his lifestyle is quite grand and not in keeping with a 12k basic income. Here's what you need to do: have a look on the back of the letter and you'll find a section that tells you how long you have to respond to the calculation if you feel it's not correct – it's usually ten days. Then write to the CMS (always by recorded delivery and then backed up by email submissions on the online portal, with each upload saved before sending too, photograph the screen if you can't work out how to do this) and say you would like a mandatory reconsideration based on 'other earned income' and state these earnings as dividends from his company and/or income from property and/or payments from shares owned and/or interest on savings and/or inheritance and/or foreign income. You can also ask them to consider hidden earnings such as assets being put into another person's name (a new partner) or a limited company he owns paying family members to defer income through them. Also state that you are willing to take the matter to tribunal if you need to and say you would like the case to be referred to the CMS Financial Investigations Unit.

Why do *you* need to do all this? Because when the CMS apply to HMRC for the non-resident parent's earnings they only provide his basic salary, not taxable income payments which come outside of this. Dreadful, isn't it? What a joke that the onus is on the resident parent to apply for this income to be taken into account, especially given his non-payment will have likely meant you have to work more to make up the shortfall. You're not exactly flush for time, I imagine. But it is what it is. If your ex works for a regular company as an employee and receives payments monthly or weekly via PAYE, then you will have a much easier time of it with the CMS.

You should also state that his lifestyle is not in keeping with the declared earnings to HMRC if this is the case. If you have evidence, provide it. Cars, holidays, home purchases (pay £3 and send in his Land Registry forms for properties he owns), etc. You have to be a bit of a sleuth because no one else will be for you, and this is for your kids. Many non-resident parents will get quite aggressive when being forced to pay for their kids. They will accuse you of greed in abusive emails and texts. Do not engage. Save all of these and send them to the CMS. Many women feel guilty when accused of being greedy and question themselves over their motives. This is what they want. You are NOT greedy. Them refusing to pay for their children is greedy. Them choosing to spend their money on other things before they contribute to the upbringing of their children is money-grabbing, selfish and immoral. It doesn't matter that you are willing and able to work doubly hard so that your children are provided for; you are doing this because the non-resident parent is not paying and so they are stealing your time with your kids as well as your money.

Getting money from your ex for the children through the CMS can be frustrating and laborious, so brace yourself if your ex is difficult. Here's how it usually works:

1. The CMS make their calculation and notify you by letter and email, you then receive payments into your bank account from your ex via 'direct pay'. You will see their name on these transactions (assuming they are paying it from their own account) and they may name the payment. Some might just pleasantly call it 'money for the children', others may name it 'mandatory payment'. Yes, really.

2. If the payments stop at any point or are late, you need to tell the CMS. They won't know until you notify them.

3. You can apply to use 'collect and pay' if payments are not regular/complete. You will need to send in evidence of these lack of payments in the form of copies of bank account statements. If your request is approved then your ex will have to pay the CMS rather than you. There is a charge for this service – you will lose 4% of your payment and your ex will have to pay a whopping extra 20%. These payments will appear in your bank account from the DWP (Department of Work and Pensions).

4. After six months of regular payments via 'collect and pay' your ex can apply to move back to direct pay. If they want to do this before six months you will have to agree to the move. However after moving back to direct pay, if they start to withhold payments again, you simply call the CMS and move back to collect and pay straight away.

5. If your ex doesn't pay the CMS via collect and pay then the CMS can apply for a DEO (deduction from earnings order), where payments are taken directly from your ex's wages, much like student loan payments are. This obviously only works if your ex has a regular job where they are an employee. If they are self-employed this is more difficult. No court order is required to do this.

6. The CMS can also apply to your ex's bank or building society to remove payments. They do not need their consent to do this and, again, no court order is required. It can be done in regular payments, or a lump sum.

7. If all else fails the CMS can take your ex to court to apply for a 'liability order'. This will only cover arrears payable and not ongoing child maintenance (I know! Because people who have arrears are so likely to pay going forwards…). A liability order is something obtained through the magistrates' court and basically admits there is a liability (money) to be paid. It gives authority to the CMS to take legal action to recover the money owed.

8. Legal action the CMS can take to ensure the money is paid includes:

- asking bailiffs to negotiate a payment, or to seize and sell belongings
- registering the debt on the Register of Judgments, Orders and Fines, making it difficult for them to get a mortgage, loan or credit card
- using an 'order for sale' to sell a property or assets, and taking the proceeds from the sale
- stopping them from getting or keeping a driving licence
- removal of their passport
- sending them to prison

In reality the CMS don't use the more draconian methods very often.

Here's something that may sound counter to the above, but hear me out. If at all possible, don't rely on your ex's child maintenance money. I'm not saying you shouldn't spend it. I know a lot of mothers save their payments in a separate bank account to give to their children when they are older. You don't have to do this. Spend it on joyous things if you wish. Or save the lot. But beware of *relying* on it. If at all possible, make it so that you never have to worry about whether or not they will pay each month. That level of control is not enjoyable to live with.

And, lastly, there's a saying that many non-paying fathers use; 'children are not pay per view'. Whilst a lot of the men who use this phrase are not doing so with the best of intentions, never stop your children from seeing their father because he hasn't paid his child maintenance. Firstly, when men don't pay, they rarely see it as punishing the child, they do it to punish the mother. Oddly many men are able to separate and compartmentalise loving their child and providing for their child. Secondly, it is not your child(ren)'s fault that their father isn't financially providing for them. They still love their dad. I don't feel it's appropriate to even tell children when their father isn't providing for them, unless they are likely to notice a significant change in their standard of living. Money is an adult subject and, frankly, telling your child that their dad is refusing to pay for them isn't hurting your ex, it's hurting your child and making them feel literally worthless. Oh and, thirdly, if the other two reasons aren't convincing, the courts do not like it if you withhold contact due to child maintenance not being paid. They do not in any way link the two and you will be viewed in a very dim light if you stop contact.

<u>Child Arrangements Order (CAO)</u>

I never thought I would end up knowing what a CAO is. I ended up being taken to court by my ex over the kids. I got a really favourable outcome. If I had my time again, I would ask for the CAO to be more buttoned down as I think too much of it was left open to interpretation and my ex seems to enjoy playing games with it. Carrie, 38.

A Child Arrangements Order is a court order that sets out who is responsible for the care of a child and is usually only sought when you and your ex can't agree on how to split the care of the children. It can be broad or extremely detailed. More on that later.

To apply for a CAO without permission from the court you must be a parent, guardian or special guardian of the child, a spouse or civil partner if the child is part of that family, someone with parental responsibility, someone who already has a residence order for that child or someone who the child has lived with for more than three years.

The process to get a CAO is very similar to the divorce process for finances, so it's worth re-reading that section. ('Legal', beginning page 47.) You will need to obtain a signed MIAM form before you can make an application for a CAO. You then fill in a C100 form (available on the government website) and complete a supplemental form C1A if you or your child have suffered, or are at risk of suffering, any harm from domestic violence or abuse, child abduction or other conduct or behaviour that could be considered harmful by your ex. It's also worth knowing that you can remove your address and contact details from any forms if you feel that you or your children will be at risk of harm if your ex has them. Instead you will need to provide your contact details to the court using a form C8.

Three copies of each form will need to be sent to the court along with the fee of £215 (unless you are exempt, in which case fill out form EX160). Remember to keep a copy for yourself and also take photos of it and keep it digitally too if you filled it in by hand. The application should be sent to the nearest court to where the children live. You can physically take the application to the court desk, queue up and pay the fee in person. Beware a lot of courts don't take cards, so cash is advisable.

Once the court receives your application, it will set a date for everyone involved in the application to have a First Hearing Dispute Resolution Appointment (FHDRA). The court will send a copy of the application to your ex, and they must complete an acknowledgement form (C7) and return it to the court to confirm that they have seen the papers. If you are on the receiving end of a C100 application, remember you need to return the C7 form no less than 10 days before the hearing. If you are concerned that there is a risk of harm to your child that the court should know about, you can complete form C1A and return this to the court at the same time as you send them the form C7.

Cafcass (the Children and Family Court Advisory and Support Service) and Cafcass Cymru (in Wales) are usually involved in most child-related disputes that go to court. The Cafcass officer's role is to provide judges with advice, information and recommendations regarding children. Their decisions are meant to be child-centric and have the children's safety in mind.

Before the first hearing Cafcass will carry out background safeguarding checks with the police and local authority (social services) to see if the children are known to them, and report to the court to highlight any safety issues. An officer from Cafcass should also contact you and your ex by phone to discuss any safety issues.

At the First Hearing, you may be able to come to an agreement which can be set out in an order (a 'consent order'), though you should not feel bullied into agreeing to anything you don't think is a good idea. If you can't agree then the judge may make a decision for you and put this into an order. Alternatively the judge may decide they need more information in order to make a decision. They may ask for statements from you and your ex, request reports from the police or social services or ask Cafcass to meet with your children to understand their wishes and feelings (a 'Section 7'). There can be several hearings to work through all the issues.

If there have been allegations of abuse, the judge may hold a fact-finding hearing and you and your ex may be cross-examined by the other party's legal representative or the judge themselves. Witnesses can be called too. The aim of a fact-finding hearing is for the judge to understand the risk and effect to the child of the abuse and determine whether either parent needs to attend a domestic violence programme.

If you cannot come to an agreement with your ex, then a final hearing will be needed. You will need to provide written statements to the court for this and you may also be required to give spoken evidence. You will be asked to take an oath or affirm (make a formal declaration) that you will tell nothing but the truth to the court and then you will have a chance to set out what you believe to be right, to the judge, for your children either yourself (if you're self-representing) or through your barrister. Your ex (if they are self-representing) or his barrister will ask you questions. The same will apply to him. The judge will reach a decision either straight away or after taking a break. This will then need to be written up into a CAO by either yours or your ex's barrister, or, if you are both self-representing, by the legal advisor at the court. The judge will sign it off and it will be a legally binding document.

Bear in mind the court are there to act in the best interests of the children and are really not interested in you or your ex and any disputes you have. You must remain calm, child-focused and remember that the court will be considering lots of areas to come to a decision. Are your children's physical, emotional and educational needs being met? Are any characteristics of the child including their age, sex and background being taken into account? Are you and your ex capable of meeting these needs? Have the children suffered at the hands of either you or your ex or are they likely to suffer? If the status quo is changed how will the children cope with that change? And in some cases, are the children's wishes and feelings being taken into account? (This will depend on the children's age and level of understanding). Everything is about the children. The judge may make you and your ex attend the Separated Parents Information Programme (SPIP); a one-off four-hour course which helps you understand how to put your children first while you are separating, even when in dispute. Its aim is to help you learn how to manage conflict and difficulties. You will not attend the course with your ex, in fact you'll have to attend separate courses. The SPIP is delivered by a number of providers at different locations across the county, on behalf of Cafcass.

Throughout this process you should be keeping an eye on what you ideally want written into the CAO. A barrister told me it's rare to get everything covered the first time and that usually parents have to live with a CAO to see the shortcomings. The kind of things you may wish to consider getting included in a CAO are:

- Who the children live with, the location and when
- When and how the children will see both parents
- Drop-off times and places for handovers
- How communication between parents will be handled; via regular email address, a dedicated email address, through a parenting app such as My Family Wizard, through a Parent Communication Book or otherwise. Will communication be within certain hours of the day, or at any time?
- If there is a significant distance between the parents, how will the travel of the children be handled?
- If a parent moves to a new house, will the address be shared with the other parent?
- What other contact will take place, either through phone calls, video calls, cards or letters?
- How long and frequent will holidays be, will the other parent be notified of holiday addresses and if so how far in advance, will there be contact during holiday periods and how?
- If the children stay away from the parents' address, will the other parent be notified of this?
- Who retains the children's passports outside of holiday periods (Did you know you don't own your children's passports even if you paid for them? So your ex can refuse to return the passports and there is very little you can do unless it's written into the CAO.)
- Provision for splitting Christmas holidays, birthdays, Mother's Day, Father's Day
- Provision for religious ceremonies, milestones and education
- Educational provision such as where the children might go to school

- Agreement on immunisations and any medical treatment required
- Safeguarding such as the children not being left alone overnight without an adult

If you know your ex is a difficult bugger then try to be as clear in the CAO as possible, because you can bet they will try and bend it otherwise. So, for example, if you have had a video call worked into the CAO on each child's birthday, with the parent they are not spending it with, you may wish to stipulate the way the video call is made – Facetime/Skype/WhatsApp. Yes I really have heard of a case where a father made the video call on Skype knowing full well that the mother's account was dormant, meaning the poor child thought his mother was ignoring his birthday call. She was patiently waiting by her phone for a Facetime or WhatsApp call. You may also wish to stipulate that the call is private and not recorded, again, yes calls have been recorded. The CAO needs to be workable and, if your ex is a dick, not open to interpretation.

A CAO usually lasts until each child is 18, unless it states otherwise, however the courts are very reluctant to enforce the 'live with' element of a CAO beyond the age of 16 unless there are exceptional circumstances. The contact arrangements set out in a CAO remain legally binding until the child reaches the age of 16 unless the order specifically states otherwise. This is in accordance with Section 91(10) of the Children Act 1989. After this point it will be up to the child to decide how much contact they would like to have with the parent they do not live with. In reality, if a child is very resistant to seeing a parent once they reach their teenage years, it is hard to make them. They have a right to be heard.

And when it comes to a CAO being upheld, I am afraid it's a civil matter rather than a police matter, so if a parent breaches it, they will be in contempt of court which could mean fines, enforcement orders, unpaid work in the community and even imprisonment (although this is extremely rare). You can apply for a CAO to be enforced using a C79 form. A hearing will usually be listed within 20 working days of the application being issued.

If you find your CAO is no longer working for you and your ex, you can deviate from it, as long as you both agree. You can also ask the court to vary an order using a C100 application, but they will only do so if they consider it to be in the best interests of the child to do so.

There is also such a thing as a Specific Issue Order (SIO); it gives directions for a specific question that has arisen, or that may arise, about any aspect of parental responsibility for a child. It can be made without a CAO if both you and your ex are happy with contact arrangements. Or it can be made with the CAO. A SIO usually covers a complex issue such as if a child:

- should be informed about their biological origins or assisted conception
- should change their gender
- can legally change their name
- can permanently relocate within the UK or abroad
- should undergo specific medical treatment or an immunisation
- should be privately educated or attend a particular school
- should change their religion

Prohibited Steps Order (PSO)

My ex-husband decided he wanted to move the children to a different school, ten miles away from where we live. He didn't want to do the school run, have more contact time or even help with the costs associated with the extra travel, he simply said he felt it would be better for the girls to be at the same school he was planning on sending his daughter to with his second wife. It all got very heated and then it went quiet until I went to pick the girls up one Friday and they were carrying leaving cards from their classes. I ended up having to go to court for a PSO which I got. He'd even told the girls not to tell me. Immie, 27.

A prohibited steps order (PSO) is a type of court order which stops a person (usually a parent) from making certain decisions about their child's upbringing or activity relating to a child(ren), and which also prohibits a party from exercising their parental responsibility. Some examples of what a PSO could prevent are a parent moving a child from their school/nursery, a child coming into contact with another person (e.g. your ex's new partner if there is good reason), the resident parent from moving a child outside of the UK or far from their current local area, one parent from changing a child's surname or a parent allowing a child to undergo risky medical treatment. A PSO is the exact opposite to a SIO as it's about preventing something from happening rather than giving permission. They are not given lightly by the court and applying for one follows almost the same process as applying for a CAO.

If the reason you are applying is regarding an imminent risk, you must make this clear to the court when you take your C100 form in. You will not need to attend a MIAM as you will be applying 'without notice' (i.e. without notifying the other party) meaning you are exempt. An example of this would be where you feel your children are at risk of abduction. In this instance you will need to take the children's passport numbers with you (if you have them) plus recent photos of your ex and children. If the judge feels they are at risk, they will order an 'all ports' warning where all airports and ports will be instructed not to allow the children to leave the UK.

Cafcass (Children and Family Court Advisory and Support Service)

I had two very different experiences with Cafcass. The first officer who interviewed me was very cold and made me feel like he thought I was a liar from the off. The second one was a really good listener and made lots of encouraging noises as I told them the situation. Maisie, 33.

Cafcass becomes involved in cases only at the request of the court, usually if parents are separating and they can't agree on what's best for their child and to try to make sure that a child or young person is kept safe. There's more information about Cafcass involvement in the CAO section (page 100).

The remit of Cafcass covers:

1. Providing judges with advice, information and recommendations regarding children.

2. Carrying out safeguarding checks with the police and the local authority (social services) to find out whether there are any known safety or welfare risks to your children.

3. Conducting telephone interviews with you and your ex to find out if either of you have any concerns about the safety and welfare of your children. (If you feel a statement from a third person is useful to your case then you can submit a statement in writing and it will become part of your case.)

4. Writing a safeguarding letter at least three days before the first hearing. It's a short report on the outcomes of the safeguarding checks and any child welfare issues raised in the telephone interviews with you and your ex.

5. Writing an 'addendum report' which is an update to the original safeguarding letter, should it be needed at subsequent hearings.

6. Working with you and your ex at the first hearing and, if there are no child protection or safeguarding concerns, trying to help you reach a safe agreement without further court proceedings. This may involve working on a parenting plan.

7. Completing a detailed Section 7 report about your children's welfare where they will often interview your children without you present (called a 'wishes and feelings' interview). These interviews will usually only be carried out if the child is 8 or older. The child can choose not to take part. Often older children prefer to 'keep out of it' in parental disputes.

Like all professions, there are good Cafcass officers and bad ones. Some are incredible at understanding the nuance and power battles at play, others just want to get the report off their desk and delivered ASAP. If Cafcass become involved in your case, here are a few bits of advice on how to handle phone and face-to-face interviews and interactions:

- Stay calm and be clear when you speak
- Be extremely respectful and do not raise your voice even if you are crying
- Be child centred in everything you say and make it clear you only want what is right for the children
- Refer to the children as 'our children' not 'my' and talk about their wishes and best interests and their rights, not yours
- Be clear what the status quo is at the moment and historically what the contact arrangements have been
- Listen to them, don't talk over them
- Do not fill silences because you feel awkward
- Don't argue or be sarcastic
- If you can think of positive things to say about your ex, don't be afraid to say them

- Don't criticise your ex as a person, if you need to be critical it should be factually based around their parenting and be about serious concerns, not differences in parenting styles
- Make notes before the meeting so that you don't forget anything important

If you want a heads up of what you will be asked by Cafcass at the first phone interview, the questions are now available online if you Google for them. It's all quite basic, glib stuff at the first interview.

And, whatever you do, if your child is to take part in a Cafcass interview about their wishes and feelings do not under any circumstances prep them for the meeting and try to influence what they say.

Another worthwhile thing to know about Cafcass; if they are involved in your child arrangements court case, you will need to ensure they are at the court on the day of each hearing. Usually there are set days for Cafcass to attend the court each week. Annoyingly courts will sometimes list a hearing date for child arrangements on days where Cafcass are not at the court, so, as soon as you have your date sent to you, call in and check. Courts can and do make administrative errors, and if your barrister is costing you £800 for the day, you'll be glad you checked Cafcass were there in advance, rather than the date having to be listed again and your legal costs doubling for no good reason.

<u>There's No Such Thing as Custody</u>

Things were very difficult in court with him. He lost his temper at one point and started saying 'they're my kids and I have a right to see them when I want' (this was because his aim of going to court was to force me to make the children available to him at any time, without prior warning). The judge was damning towards him and said 'they're not your children, they are both of your children and it's their right to spend time with their parents, not yours'. I thought my ex was going to explode. He didn't get what he wanted, because it wasn't workable. I have to work, and the children have a routine. Plus the older ones have lives of their own with clubs and groups they attend regularly. He said he couldn't commit to seeing them every week at the same time due to his work commitments (unlikely) and really cut his nose off to spite his face. He only sees them twice a month now, and it's all of his own making. Diane, 45.

Children are not possessions owned by one parent or another. You do not have 'custody' of them or 'access' to them. The family courts don't use these terms and I'd suggest you don't either. There is such a thing as 'residency' now and 'contact' - where the children live and who they spend time with. The focus in family law is always on the children and their rights. Not yours as a parent. If you end up in the family court over your kids you must always talk about what is best for the children, what they want and their rights. Not yours. Reference them as 'our children' not 'my children' verbally and in all documents.

Daddy Says…(What is Parental Alienation?)

The kids came back from their weekend with him and were really off with me. I knew something had happened but have learnt to let them tell me things in their own time. Badgering them shuts them down. It was when I was bathing my youngest son that night, only 5 years old, that he looked at me really intensely and said, 'Daddy says that you made him leave us and that you have taken all his money and his house and that he can't afford to take us out for ice creams because of you.' You could have knocked me down with a feather. This was so far from the truth, my instinct was to defend myself in anger. What daddy hadn't explained was that daddy had been addicted to online gambling and had taken out credit cards in both our names and saddled me with a lot of joint debt. I was so, so angry with him for discussing the break-up with our little ones, especially discussing it and misrepresenting me. I garbled an explanation about how mummy and daddy both loved him and his sisters very much but that there were some things that meant mummy felt she didn't want to live with daddy anymore, and that daddy shouldn't discuss money with children. I don't know if I did the right thing, but, honestly, I didn't know what to say. I sent him a really shitty email telling him to stop lying to the kids, which of course he didn't even respond to. Daisy, 38.

Parental alienation is a buzz word in the family courts at the moment. Parental alienation is defined by Cafcass as:

'While there is no single definition, we recognise parental alienation as when a child's resistance or hostility towards one parent is not justified and is the result of psychological manipulation by the other parent.'

What this means is anything one parent is saying or doing to negatively influence their children against the other parent. It can be obtuse in its nature ('your mum's a slag and had an affair, if she loved you she wouldn't have done that), or it can be covert, such as being clear that any mention of the other parent is forbidden. It's often somewhere in the middle, mild 'negging' of the other parent, comments about stealing money, houses, possessions etc.

It's a very tricky area because children often have questions about their parents and the nature of the separation, and those questions are often directed at the parent they feel most secure and comfortable with.

So, in separations where there's abuse, the child may ask the parent who has been abused and left the family home, why dad says mum is a bitch and has ruined his life. What do you say? First check your face and your expressions, because they can and will betray you. Do your best Oscar-winning performance and say calmly that dad has some feelings about mum which he really should not be sharing with his kids, and that dad's opinions are his to have, but not to share. That you hope dad will come to feel a bit less angry in the future and that you are sorry that your child had to hear this. And that you love them. You must hold your nerve. Do not sling mud. Do not ask your child to take sides. Remember that your child is half of their father and that if you say negative things about their dad, you are saying negative things about your son or daughter. They still identify as being part of their parents; don't make them hate themselves. If you say negative things about their dad, you are telling them that they are innately bad *and* that they love a bad person. Imagine the years of therapy they will need.

You can and should say absolutely anything you want about your ex, but not to your kids. And if your ex is not as kind, then remember you can't control their actions. Just remind your children that they should not be brought into adult arguments, that it is unfair to say bad things about mummy to them, but leave it there. This is a long, long journey you are on. You have to hope that your ex will have a personality transplant and be kind and loving in the future. If this doesn't happen, you have to reduce the damage to your kids.

<u>Surnames</u>

I want to change my surname but at the moment the twins are young and I don't want to confuse them so I'm keeping my married name. As soon as they're at secondary school I feel it'll be the right time to change it. Jada, 32.

You either feel strongly about this or you don't. Me? Well I had already established myself career-wise with my married name, so I've kept it. At some point in the future, I may change it, never say never. Whatever decision you make, don't be influenced by older relatives who are often quite traditional about names. You choose your name, no one else.

Changing back to your maiden name is very simple. You will need copies of your birth certificate, marriage certificate, a signed statement to say you are changing back to your maiden name for all purposes and your decree absolute. These will then be used by the passport office, the DVLA, banks, service providers etc. Of course there will be a charge associated with some of them (a new passport, for sure). You can alternatively change your name by Deed Poll too; there is a free service online and also paid-for services.

Triggered

When my youngest comes back from his dad's, I have to make sure we have something planned where it's passive. All it takes is one Saturday with him and he sounds like him, copies his mannerisms and even adopts his point of view on some contentious subjects. I find it hugely triggering as these were the reasons we split. It doesn't help that he's the spit of his dad. Lucia, 37.

When children live between two homes, they learn to adapt quickly to different house rules, parenting styles, menus, even politics. And the easiest way to navigate this for a lot of children is to imitate. So your child skips off to see their father as their true self (or at least the true self you experience of them), but returns parroting their dad, with their mannerisms and demeanour. It can be very triggering of bad memories. I'd hazard a guess that your ex may feel the same when they first arrive at his house too. Upon returning to you, try to allow them decompression time without interaction. This might be playing on iPads, reading a book, building Lego in their room. Whatever it is, encourage something they can enjoy alone in the readjustment period.

Step Mums

The affair I could cope with, the jealousy subsided in the end. The adoration of their new 'step mum' was so much harder. I felt like my heart was breaking when they came home with tales of Beth this and Beth that. They're my world and I never expected to have to share them with another woman whilst they were so young. Melissa, 31.

Oh it hurts. I know. I will never forget the physical stabbing sensation I felt in my ovaries the evening after the boys told me they had spent their weekend making Mother's Day cards for their step mum. It felt raw, a labour-like pain, pulsating and coming in waves. I didn't want it. I could barely believe it; how did my body know? And, my, it hurt! It's okay to feel that pain and understand that it's not an unnatural reaction; these are the babies you raised. But it must be kept secret from the children because, actually, their ability to show love and care for other people who look after them is testament to what great children they are. It's a win, not a loss. That doesn't make it less hard, but it's nothing they should be made to feel guilty for.

If things aren't amicable with your ex and his new partner and it feels like a struggle to smile sweetly as your babies wax lyrical about her, remember that love is infinite. If you have more than one child, you didn't love the first born less when the second came along, did you? Your love grew. And, likewise, your child loving another woman as a caregiver does not mean they love you less.

Wicked Step Mums

I don't know what I expected from a 22 year old but his new girlfriend is not great with the girls. She seems to enjoy dressing the younger two up and plaiting their hair but she doesn't cope well with our eldest daughter who is 14. She competes with her and makes sly comments to her about me. Safe to say, our eldest hates her with a passion. I thought I'd be pleased about this but, to be honest, it gives me no pleasure. It's making contact weekends a nightmare as the eldest whips the other two up into not wanting to go and, frankly, I need a break. Tori, 43.

Stepmothers have a really hard role. They're kind of set up to fail, aren't they? Always compared to their partner's ex and having to find a slot in family dynamics that are well established. Never the 'real' mum. If you find yourself in a situation where the step mum isn't being her best self to your children, playing the 'choose me' game with your ex, try to feel some kindness to her as your first response. Only a very insecure person tries to get between a parent and their child, so she is obviously feeling worried her relationship is fragile and not able to withstand big parental love.

If you have an amicable relationship with your ex, you can try to broach the subject with him. Beware, you have to handle this with huge diplomacy. Approach it as you might imagine someone talking to him about issues with you when you were married. It's *that* tricky. He will likely see it as an attack and be defensive, assuming you are jealous or trying to cause problems in his relationship. It needs to be done in a really sensitive manner; if you feel you can't do this, avoid.

If your children are old enough you can help them with tools to navigate the situation. You might equip them with how to talk to their dad about their feelings, give them ideas of how to find common ground with their stepmother. Remember too that a lot of children feel such loyalty to their mother they will initially resist a relationship with a new step mum. You can assure them that you don't mind if they enjoy spending time with their dad's new partner and that if they're happy, you're happy.

Obviously if there's abuse none of the above applies and you will need to seek advice from a solicitor or other legal advisor on how to proceed. As with any abusive situation you should keep all evidence. See the chapter on abuse (page 117) for more general information.

<u>Giving Your Children a Love Story</u>

As a little girl, I loved my mum recounting the love story of how her and my dad met. It was magical to know you'd come from such romance! I feel like my daughter is denied that. Sure, she has the love story of how we met, but she also has a two-year court battle, numerous arguments over child maintenance and an overwhelming feeling of (as she puts it) 'Daddy just hates you, mummy'. Lara, 34.

I wrestled with this one. My ex-husband and I got engaged nine days after meeting, quite a love story, huh? It would have been a proper braggy story for our kids if it had lasted. I used to dine out on it myself! It all ending in divorce just shy of nine years later isn't quite the fairy-tale ending to the story people want to hear.

When parents divorce, the children often miss out on a positive narrative of how they came to exist. The way of the world is that we don't reward love stories unless they end in death (!), anything that ends otherwise is a non-love story. I have tried very hard to reassure my sons that their mum and dad, though not in love anymore, did love each other very much indeed and that we were so excited when we found out we were expecting every one of them.

Instead of telling your children the fairy-tale story of how mummy met daddy and they lived happily ever after, you can make your children the centre of their own fairy tale. Something like this:

'Once upon a time, it was a dark and stormy night and mummy could feel you wriggling in her tummy. She knew it was time for you to meet mummy and daddy and so we went to the hospital and when we first saw your beautiful eyes, we fell in love and couldn't imagine how we had ever existed before you…'

Children Love Traditional

I've been seeing Ben now for just over three years and we're planning for him to move in soon. My sons who are both in their early teens are desperate for us to marry. I was really surprised at how traditional they are about it. I did wonder if it was some hankering for stability but they know marriage is no guarantee after what happened with their father. Felicity, 50.

It's what they consume, isn't it? In TV, films, books…it's the norm and if there's one thing that children with divorced parents want is to be like everybody else. And it isn't just children either, is it? Parents, siblings, friends. You can bet if they're married themselves or widowed, they will be in huge favour of you running down that aisle again.

I sometimes have romantic notions of getting married again; I think about how happy it would make one of the boys in particular. But it's not what I want, so I can't give them that Disney version of a family. And let's remember, with almost all 'perfect' families, if you delve back far enough there are secrets and lies and skeletons to be found. No family is perfect. And in my flawed, not very traditional family, I have found there's a lot of beauty in the imperfections.

Cock Before Flock

I hate that he prioritises his Tinder dates over the children. Hate it so much. He has cancelled on them more than once because he wants to get laid – I know because he posts on social media when he's out. Bloody fool. He even took them on a couple of daytime dates with women who have kids. I could scream sometimes at how much he annoys me. Amber, 28.

Really shitty behaviour, putting your cock before your flock (as my pal Soph calls it). You can't change him (you know that). What you can do is congratulate yourself at not being in a relationship with a man who isn't able to prioritise as an adult should. It is hard on kids to be on the receiving end, but there are ways to mitigate the effects of his behaviour. One woman told me that once she realised her ex was cancelling because he didn't want his sons overnight (meaning he couldn't pick up women), she suggested they just hang out for the day and then he bring them back. He sees them more now than before and whilst it doesn't give her the overnight break she craves, it does stop her sons feeling disposable.

One Day

My grandmother is brilliant. When I was in a really low period after the split and beating myself up about how my daughters will cope with being from a broken home, she stopped me and said, 'you know they don't stay young forever? One day they'll leave, and you better not still be crying.' I told you she was brilliant! Laura, 29.

One day, far in the future and also in the blink of an eye, your kids won't always be your whole life. I know that's hard to imagine. But think of your own parents, are you their whole life since you left home? I doubt it.

They will go out into the world and have their own lives and so too will you. I think of these younger years of mothering as putting gas in the tank. I have spent many hours playing games, helping with homework, mopping a feverish brow and making packed lunches. Has it all been scintillating? No. Have I felt like I was losing my mind at times to the wiping and the folding and the tidying? Yes. Has it been important work to anchor my children steadily and shore them up for what life may throw at them? God, yes.

Single mothering is hard work. It's double mothering. But when they go, my time will be freer again, and a new day will start that will be less about their needs. What I am saying, albeit not succinctly, is that the focus should rightly be on your children, but don't lose sight of the very near future when they will not be your whole world.

Chapter 6

Abuse

We went to my parents for Sunday lunch and I thought we were having a nice time. The kids were upstairs with my dad and my mum was in the lounge with us. My husband was fiddling with a Playmobil car, I think trying to put a wing mirror back on. It was just a very boring, normal Sunday. I asked him if he fancied stopping off to feed the ducks on the way home and he didn't seem to hear me. I asked him again, a little louder, thinking maybe I didn't speak loudly enough. Still nothing. My mum gave me a look, an 'is everything okay' look. I felt such shame because this wasn't unusual in public. He didn't do it at home, mind. We packed the kids and the toys into the car and I asked him why he hadn't answered me. He said, 'I was busy.' I cried as we drove home. I had never felt so insignificant. Ali, 37.

Just because the law is only just catching up on varying definitions of abuse, it doesn't mean they are finite. Until recently coercive control was not illegal. It now is. I want to open your mind to what abuse is because when you are in it, it is your normal and therefore harder to accept.

If your partner tries to strangle you, most women will know this is abusive and whether they take action or not, are aware it is wrong. Likewise, if your spouse slaps you, punches you, kicks you, throws things at you. But not all abuse is bloody.

If a woman finds herself selling her old clothes on eBay when pregnant due to having little or no funds, yet her partner is spending freely on non-essentials, this is abusive. If your spouse denies saying something or doing something when it did actually happen, blaming you, this is abusive. It is called gaslighting. If your spouse drives aggressively, at speed, when you disagree with them about something whilst on a journey, this is abuse. If your spouse makes you do things sexually that you don't want to do and you feel unable to tell them or you do and they ignore it, this is abuse. If your partner refuses to speak to you, ignores you, consigns you to a cell of silence, this is abuse. If your spouse controls what you eat, this is abuse. I could go on. In short, if it's something you are uncomfortable with and you feel powerless to stop it, it's a form of abuse.

Abuse is a many-headed beast, and when the power in a relationship starts to be weighed in one person's favour, it tends to start tipping more and more. There's a snowball effect as one person becomes stronger, the other weakens. So that one day you wake up and cannot believe this miserable life you are leading belongs to you.

Not identifying with being a victim is one of the key reasons victims stay in their situations. To admit you have been abused labels you into a category that's a club you really don't want to be a member of. I get it. You don't have to become a campaigner for domestic abuse. But you do owe it to yourself to get out. (NB: You will need specialist advice about leaving an abuser, please speak to The National Domestic Abuse Helpline and/or Women's Aid about planning to leave. Their websites are www.nationaldahelpline.org.uk and www.womensaid.org.uk). And if you have kids, you owe it to them too. It is one thing to feel as though *you* don't have options, as victims of domestic abuse so often experience. It is altogether another thing to not have any options other than running away, as a child so often does. You have to wear the big pants even when you are pained. That is motherhood.

They Don't Take Out an Ad

I am a Dr of physics, a high earner and someone who considers herself to be emotionally astute. It still shocks me that I didn't see him for what he was. He was emotionally extremely abusive. I won't go into details as it's very outing, but I feel shame for the depths he sank to. I know it's not my shame to hold. I should have left years earlier, but it was a bit like the boiling frog effect. It happened so slowly and incrementally that I didn't notice how bad it was until I found myself on the phone to the Samaritans one night. Petra, 45.

Don't feel guilty for not seeing an abuser, they don't bloody advertise it! They are masters of disguise. After you have left, if you find yourself feeling guilt and shame for staying with the abuser you need to do a few things. First, access some therapy. Second, look into doing the Freedom Programme (www.freedomprogramme.co.uk). Third, make a commitment to yourself to notice red flags in future relationships (see page 121). If you don't trust yourself then ask a trusted friend to hold you accountable.

Flight, Fight, Freeze, Flop, Fawn

I am constantly saying sorry to everyone, I do it without thinking. It started when I was married to my ex. He would shout at me over little things and once we had a baby I started to apologise before he started shouting, so that he didn't wake the baby up. It escalated, of course, as these things do. He pushed me into the garage wall one afternoon and I found myself later comforting him and explaining to him that it's no wonder he pushed me given how annoying I was being. I had this weird flash-forward to seeing our daughter being pushed and shoved by her own husband and knew it had to stop. Lennie, 34.

Being in an abusive relationship is traumatic. There are five main responses to trauma, all reactions we have in common with animals. They're all ways we adapt to survive a threatening situation.

1. Fight

Quite simply, we're in a dangerous situation so we fight to defend ourselves. This can be literal physical fighting or verbal fighting.

2. Flight

In a dangerous situation, we flee in order to keep ourselves safe.

3. Freeze

This is a survival reaction where the whole body becomes temporarily frozen or numb. Muscles tighten, the body feels paralysed. In nature it's a play-dead response. Freezing is a sign that the brain can't process what's happening so it goes into shock until it decides what to do next.

4. Flop

Another survival reaction which might involve blacking out, collapsing, losing control of your bodily functions or losing consciousness. Your muscles become floppy and inert.

5. Fawn

This is where survival is dependent on submitting to the threat in order to survive; for example maintaining a good relationship with the abuser. The victim placates the person threatening them by trying to please them or being their friend. This is a common response with domestic abuse, hostage situations, sexual abuse, childhood abuse and torture.

The fawn response is extremely common for women who are living with their abuser, especially where there are children and pets in the house too. The woman will keep the peace to mitigate any further abuse to them, their children or to the family pet.

If you have been in an abusive relationship, it's likely some of your learnt survival-based trauma responses will spill over into how you communicate with other people in your life. Being someone who fawns makes you vulnerable to narcissists (see Chapter 7, page 135) in future relationships. Key signs you're stuck in the fawn response are:

1. Feeling other people's needs are more important than yours.

2. Always apologising even when there's no need.

3. Feeling unable to say if you're having a hard time to other people by being overly positive in order not to burden them.

4. Paying excessive compliments to others often without any justification.

5. Being extremely enthusiastic in emails and texts by using a lot of happy emojis or exclamation marks just to ensure you're always perceived as happy and easy-going.

There are things you can do to help you move away from this fawning habit. The best thing to do (as ever) is to seek therapy for re-enacting your trauma responses. If you can't do this for any reason, you can make a conscious effort to make small changes. First things first, banish 'sorry' from your vocabulary. Find a way to apologise, if you need to, that isn't as submissive as a 'sorry'. If you feel you've kept someone waiting, say 'thank you for waiting for me', for example. Practise saying no in private, without the need to give elaborate reasons for it. (Check out Learning To Say No, page 24 for ideas). Tell a trusted friend that you have been pretending everything is okay, even when it isn't. And if you're an over user of emojis and exclamation marks, wean yourself off them gently. People will be so used to your exuberant communications if you abruptly stop using them you may spark concerns of terminal illness and the like.

<u>Red Flags</u>

On our first date he took me through a whistlestop tour of every 'mad ex' of his. I look back now and realise this was a huge red flag. Five years, a marriage and one child later I can confirm that it was in fact him who made me mad, and the others too, I'd guess. Lori, 27.

I could write an entire book on red flags to look out for. There are so many ways a person shows you who they are. You must listen to them, as the signs are almost always there. Read through Listening, page 6 for more on this.

You may have ignored some major red flags in your marriage, but, moving forward you can decide not to ignore them in future relationships. Here are a few of the clangers to be vigilant of:

1. He says all his exes are crazy, mad, mental etc. The common theme here is him. If it *is* true, then he is clearly the person sending these women 'crazy', and why would you want to be a part of this unfortunate gang? If it's not true, why would you want to be with a man who describes all his exes in such a derogatory way?

2. They don't want to share you with your family and friends, even your work. Why? He knows that anyone not in those first flushed stages of love might see that he's a wrong 'un and out him.

3. They accelerate the relationship. They tell you they love you, want to marry you, propose even, suggest you have a baby, want to move in and generally push you into a very committed relationship fast. This is love bombing. Check out a full explanation on this in Love Bombing, page 143.

4. They push your boundaries, physically and otherwise. He might tickle you even though you have told him you hate it, he may check your emails saying this is what committed people do, he may put a tracker on your phone so that he can make sure he has a cup of tea ready for you just as you get home, he may suggest you have a threesome or that you try 'breath-play' during sex, he may suggest an open relationship, he may call you repeatedly if he can't get hold of you immediately. Whatever it is, if it makes you uncomfortable and you feel you have no control over the pushing of the boundary, this is a red flag.

5. They make fun of you. This might be outright public humiliation. Or it might be negging. What's negging? Giving a compliment whilst also putting you down, for example, 'you look really pretty when you wear make-up' or 'I am so pleased you got the promotion, do you think your boss fancies you?' or 'sex last night was amazing, I wish it could be like that all the time'. It might also be done in private, perhaps about you being less educated than him or less cultured. It's often around sex; suggesting your techniques are

poor, that you are not very adventurous. The aim is to wear you down so that your self-esteem is so low, you won't stray.

6. They name call. In arguments they call you names rather than have a row about the issue at hand. They often call others names too. Their boss is a 'fucking moron'. Their mother 'a stupid bitch'. Other drivers are 'twats, silly bitches'. A lot of the name-calling will be specific to women – slags, bitches, whores, cows, cunts etc.

7. They are cruel or unpleasant to their parents and/or animals. Obviously, many people have complicated relationships with their parents, but if he is cruel this is a red flag. A toxic relationship with a parent can be navigated without cruelty, even if it involves going no contact. Cruelty to animals is even more concerning and is accepted as a marker of being a psychopath.

8. They are lazy, work-shy and poor with money. You do not need a dependant to care for, cajole, find a job for and pay for. You need an equal partner who contributes like an adult. You would not put up with a friend who relied on you to pay for everything, don't let this happen in a romantic relationship.

9. They are liars. The lies might be huge, like saying they are divorced when they are still married. Or they might be small like saying they stopped off to buy a bottle of wine on the way home but the shop was shut when actually they didn't stop at all. The lies might have been something you were involved in, like him cheating on his ex with you. Liars are addicted to their creation of the truth and the more lies they tell, the more they have to tell. It cascades until they (and you if you are in a relationship with them) are living in an alternative reality.

10. They want to keep your relationship a secret. Why? This isn't romantic or exciting. He feels ashamed of being in a relationship with you. You deserve better than that.

11. They never apologise. Apologising in a relationship is important. We all do and say things that we wish we hadn't and we need to be able to admit we are fallible and apologise (and, crucially, change our behaviour). If he doesn't apologise or makes a non-apology where he blames you ('I'm sorry you're upset') run for the hills.

12. They abuse people, animals and/or things. This is an umbrella red flag for hitting you, your children or pets, slapping, shouting, fighting on nights out, kicking doors, punching holes in walls, throwing things at you or at the wall, abusing or being addicted to alcohol/drugs/gambling/sex workers/affairs/sexting.

13. They don't support their kids. If they have children and are not paying child maintenance, or only pay under duress, ask yourself if this is a good man you want to make a life with. Also consider how he might behave if you had a child together. People rarely change.

14. You find yourself making excuses for them. When others can see how awful they are and bring this to your attention, you make excuses or lie about their behaviour.

Controlling the Abuser

I don't recognise who I became when I was with him. I found ways to control him without him knowing, to kind of stop him getting to the point where he was angry. He didn't ever hit me, but his words and shouting could be as vicious as a slap. I look back now and realise there was something very wrong when you're married to a man who when he accidentally drives on the wrong side of the road on holiday, rather than tell him straight away, you gently suggest that you would easily make this mistake if you too were distracted by naughty children and the car air con not working. Yes, that happened. I put all our lives at risk to stop him from losing his rag with me for correcting him from driving on the left in Spain. Selma, 34.

When you are in an abusive relationship (whether physically abused, coercively controlled, or any other form) you will naturally seek ways to mitigate the abuse, and one of these methods is through learning to manipulate and control your abuser. It's something an abuser will accuse their partner of to make them feel shame and guilt for contributing to the abusive situation.

There is no shame in having learnt to control your abuser in order to lessen their impact. It does not make you part of the problem; it's a survival tool.

Trauma Busying

I couldn't stop being busy. I was constantly rearranging the house, tidying, moving items from one room to another, then off to the shops for something minor three times a day, off to a friend's to post a newspaper article through their door I thought they would enjoy. I couldn't stop walking. Everywhere. I even walked into town on the Saturdays he had the kids. I would walk for ninety minutes to get there, walk around the shops browsing and then walk home. Scarlett, 31.

This busy behaviour is a coping mechanism experienced by a lot of women. A need to walk, clean, tidy, jog, swim the trauma out of their bodies. The activity becomes both a symptom and a good coping mechanism for post-traumatic stress disorder (PTSD) (see page 129) which a lot of women experience within and after an unhappy marriage. At the height of stressful litigation, I wore a pedometer one day to track my steps and was shocked to see I was walking 12,000 steps just within my home. I knew if I slowed down, I had to face my feelings and confront the truth.

Trauma Consumption

When I was married, I never missed an episode of EastEnders. *My ex-husband hated it and would sigh and ridicule me for watching what he saw as a low-rent soap. He said it was depressing. He was right! But I felt such affinity with the characters because I was miserable like them. Funny thing is I haven't watched it once since he left. Hadhira, 32.*

When you are in a traumatic situation, you will often seek trauma in your consumption. Traumatic films, biographies about people who have been abused, music about bad men and heartache. It makes you feel less alone. There is comfort in seeing others in your world. Don't be surprised if your tastes change gradually or abruptly once you leave a traumatic relationship.

DARVO

I stopped calling him out on his behaviour as I knew if I did, he would turn it around. Whenever I challenged him, I would be the one to end up apologising. Cedella, 47.

This acronym stands for Deny, Attack, and Reverse Victim and Offender and was created by a professor of psychology called Jennifer J Freyd in 1997.

It's a strategy used by abusers to disarm anyone calling them out on their behaviour. Here's how it works:

1. DENY The abuser denies what they're accused of. For example 'I didn't say that' or 'I wasn't flirting' etc. Essentially this is gaslighting (see page 148) where the abuser denies that someone else's lived reality took place.

2. ATTACK The abuser then attacks. They will turn the criticism around and focus the blame on the person calling them out. For example 'you're jealous', 'you're mental', 'you're imagining things', 'you're sneaky looking at my phone' and even 'be careful what you say, that's slander'. Sometimes these attacks are violent.

3. REVERSE the roles of VICTIM and OFFENDER The shift of attention has moved from the abuser to you. It's been reversed. You're now starting to feel guilt as you are blamed for having questioned the abuser's behaviour, the abuser is now the victim. They may cry, act as if they are profoundly hurt and distressed by what you've suggested. They may be silent and refuse to talk to you or become extremely aggressive in a guise of defending themselves as the victim. For example, 'you're making me feel bullied', or 'I can't believe you're accusing me of having an affair when you know my dad did that to my mum and I never got over it'. The horror is complete; the abuser has turned the whole scene around and you are now the offender. You may find yourself justifying why you questioned him, apologising for doubting him and even thinking you are losing your mind given you might have concrete evidence of the behaviour you are calling out. You will likely end up consoling your abuser and even seeking to make amends through affection, sex, gifts or other acts of service.

DARVO is something an abuser uses to stop you from making further criticisms because the result is confusing, painful and guilt-inducing. It's very clever. It's highly unlikely it's done knowingly; as in the abuser doesn't think 'ah this is a great opportunity for my old pal DARVO'. It's just something they naturally do to deflect and blame.

<u>Drama Triangle</u>

The dynamic in our family was very unhealthy. I was really shouty and quite horrible to my daughter when we were married. I would lose my temper with her and often raise my voice on purpose to summon him to come and see what was going on. Then once he came into the room, she would act like I was evil, sob hysterically and sometimes cower (which she never did until he arrived – I wasn't that bad!) and he would rescue her from me. Once I asked him to leave, this all stopped. Leona, 44.

The drama (or rescue) triangle doesn't just exist in romantic relationships, it can occur in any form of relationship, often multi-generationally in families. Put simply it's where roles are played within a triangle; one person acts as a victim, one as a rescuer and one as a persecutor. It was recognised and named by Stephen Karpman over 40 years ago and is a dynamic a lot of us will have been a part of. The roles are parasitic and interchangeable, so the person who is the rescuer may at points become the victim and so on.

1. The victim. They see themselves as powerless, hopeless, ashamed, needing special treatment. They cannot accept responsibility for their situation and feel unable to change their circumstances. They seek a rescuer to save them though will view that person as a persecutor if they refuse/fail to rescue them.

2. The rescuer. They want to help and often derive much pleasure and joy from helping the victim. They will often neglect themselves in order to do this. They are co-dependent, in that they need the victim in order to get their sense of worth. They are often enablers, as they may not want the victim to change their circumstances and stop needing them. They can experience guilt when not playing their martyr role, though can also experience resentment because of the commitment required of this role.

3. The persecutor. They are critical and blaming of the victim, often angry and unpleasant. They'll make the victim feel bad about their situation by issuing threats and bullying them without offering any help in solving the problem the victim has. They are fearful of becoming the victim themselves so will be careful not to show vulnerability for fear of the tables turning.

The way this plays out in relationships is rarely as extreme as these descriptions, but it's helpful to see them in these pen portrait caricatures so you can spot who's who. There's much drama in this interchangeable triangular dynamic; the victims get to be cared for, the rescuers get to feel useful and the persecutors get to feel superior to both. You'll notice where there are substance abuse issues within a relationship or family, this triangle is often at play.

Sunken Cost Fallacy

I meant to leave when the children were young, but I put it off. Then I meant to leave when they were at uni and I decided to wait a while because after being together for so long it seemed silly to split up. Then, once the children started to get engaged, I didn't want to ruin the weddings with a broken family. And then the grandchildren arrived and that seemed like a bad time too. One day I was walking past some shops and I saw this woman in the window who was old and looked very unhappy and stooped. It was me! I decided there and then I had to leave him. He's been a really horrible husband and despite the fact I am now well into my sixties, I am grabbing life with both hands. I wish I had done it sooner. If you are putting it off, be careful, life passes really quickly. The days are long but the years are short. Valerie, 67.

Heard of the sunken cost fallacy? It's where a person carries on with a behaviour or situation (such as marriage) because of the amount they have already invested in it. This might be time, money or effort. When it comes to marriage, it's often all three.

There are definitely reasons for putting off a separation or divorce, but if you find yourself feeling you may as well stay, despite being deeply unhappy, because you've already done 20 years, it might be time to have a long, hard think.

Evidence

If there's one bit of advice I would give you it's to keep everything. If he sends a nasty email, print it off and keep it, save a PDF of it too. Same for texts – take photos of them and save the pictures away from your phone. If he turns up at the house after you've asked him not to, video it and take pictures. If it escalates you need all this. India, 39.

If your husband/ex-husband is abusing you in any way, keep all evidence. If his abuse is written, keep copies of it. If you're unlucky enough to have been physically hurt, document it immediately with photos but also by seeing a medical professional so that it's recorded in your medical files. Keeping a diary of everything is essential as you will forget the details over time.

Get specialist advice from The National Domestic Abuse Helpline and/or Women's Aid about how you can plan an escape. Their websites are www.nationaldahelpline.org.uk and www.womensaid.org.uk. If you are at immediate risk call 999 for the police.

Leaving an Abusive Relationship

I tried to leave three times before I actually did. Each time he convinced me to come back and try again. He said he'd changed. He never did. I was so optimistic. In the end I had to leave without him knowing, it was planned for months. I saved money, I had a place to go to, everything was sorted in advance. It's the hardest and best thing I ever did. Miranda, 40.

Leaving a relationship that isn't abusive is hard, to leave one that is requires Herculean effort. Being abused damages your self-esteem so that your belief that you can cope alone is very low. You may well be isolated, have restricted access to money, transport, friends and family. You may feel ashamed of the situation you are in and be embarrassed. You may still hold out hope that your abuser will change or feel bound by your religion to stay in the relationship.

Getting specialist advice about leaving an abusive relationship is important. It is NOT like leaving a regular relationship. The stakes are higher. The reason women fear leaving an abusive relationship isn't a neurotic baseless worry, it's because it's a dangerous thing to do. There is a huge rise in the likelihood of violence after separating from an abuser. 41% of women killed by a male partner/former partner in England, Wales and Northern Ireland in 2018 had separated or taken steps to separate from them. (Femicide Census, 2020). The National Domestic Abuse Helpline and/or Women's Aid can help you plan how to leave, including how to cover your tracks online and in real life. Their websites are www.nationaldahelpline.org.uk and www.womensaid.org.uk. Remember that the majority of women in an abusive relationship try to leave multiple times before they manage it, so if you have tried before and not managed to, it doesn't mean you won't in the future.

Post-Traumatic Stress Disorder (PTSD)

I have this irrational fear of the postman. Well I suppose it's not irrational given my ex-husband used to get his solicitor to send me multiple letters, usually on a Friday when I had no way to get any legal advice quickly before the weekend. God it was an awful time. Even now when my four year old shouts, 'Mummy! Post!' in her excitement at the letterbox shutter sound, my stomach flips. I leave post unopened for long periods of time as it makes me feel very unwell opening it. I'm talking shaking and feelings of proper doom. I am going to go and talk to someone about it as I don't even like opening the door to the postman anymore. Veronica, 38.

PTSD is usually associated with war, road traffic accidents and violent crimes, but it can also come from experiences of loss, including, of course, divorce. PTSD is described as living in a state of high alert, in fear. Symptoms can include (but are not limited to) feelings of numbness, emptiness, anxiousness, intense feelings of distress at reminders of the trauma, night terrors, flashbacks, intrusive thoughts, excessive worrying, panic attacks, trembling, vomiting, sweating, diarrhoea, feeling jumpy and irritable, being easily startled, needing to keep busy, episodes of anger, feeling unable to trust anyone, using alcohol or drugs to cope with difficult memories, having problems focusing, dizziness and headaches.

PTSD from an abusive marriage can feel like lacking a credible witness; you don't trust the only other person who knows what happened as they were the abuser. But you don't trust your own memories either, so you're left with confusion and a sense of unreliability. PTSD can feel like an all-consuming whole body and mind experience, because when we're stressed emotionally, our bodies release the hormones cortisol and adrenaline. This is the body's automatic way of preparing to respond to a threat, sometimes called the 'fight or flight' response (see page 119 for more on this). Really helpful at times, but when you need to function on a daily basis it can be debilitating.

One of the problems with a traumatic divorce where there are children involved is that in most cases it will be necessary to have ongoing contact with your ex throughout the divorce process and beyond. It can be hard to make peace with this. If you suspect you're suffering from PTSD, see your GP to access some help.

Abuse Through Marriage Counselling

I wish we hadn't gone to couples counselling together. It was absolutely awful and even more traumatic than some of the abuse within the marriage. I thought the counsellor would see through him but she ended up siding with him and I felt very bullied. I was let down by her and now realise since accessing some great one-on-one therapy that you should never go for counselling with an abuser. Dee, 55.

Couples counselling relies on both parties wanting equality within the relationship. If one person is abusing the other, it simply can't work as the abuser is not committed to an equal relationship to start with. Even worse, the fact that the person being abused is engaging in counselling and therefore taking a portion of responsibility for the abuse, gives the abuser the excuse that their partner is complicit in their mistreatment. Essentially, that the victim's behaviour is part of the reason they abuse. This is never the case; abuse is not deserved or provoked, it is a choice the abuser makes.

Some therapists can become manipulated by the abuser and help them to coercively control the victim. Never assume a therapist or counsellor is not open to being hoodwinked by the abuser, they absolutely are. Abusers can be extremely charming and use this to manipulate others. Think back to when you met your abuser; were they abusive from day one?

It's also common for the abuser to use disclosures made in couples counselling at a later date, particularly weaponising them in court or telling children/colleagues/family/friends private details. You must play your cards close to your chest with an abuser.

Abuse Through Litigation

I lost control of my bowels at a children's theme park after reading an email from my ex's solicitor, such was the content. Funny in hindsight, having to wash my trousers in the sink of the loos and dry them under a hand dryer whilst my toddler said, 'Mummy, it smells bad in here' at the top of her voice, but bloody awful at the time. A stark reminder of the power he still had over me. Rebecca, 31.

I need to mention this as I believe in the future it will be legislated against. When you're divorcing an abusive spouse and they have reached all possible dead ends in abusing you emotionally, physically or financially, they really only have one option left to them; abuse through litigation. And please know that this amazingly encompasses all areas of abuse; receiving daily letters from your ex's solicitor, court summons, applications for a non-molestation order, applications for your children to live with them, evidence in the form of outright lies, and bent out of context truths.

If your ex has access to unlimited funds, then abuse through litigation can be a very enjoyable and socially acceptable way to terrorise. Don't underestimate the effect of it. If you are receiving multiple solicitor's letters, then know this; you do not have to reply to them. There is no legal obligation to reply to solicitor's letters. With court applications, if you find you are at the end of repeated court applications then you can apply for something called a Section 91 (14) barring order which essentially means that the other party will not be able to make a court application without permission from a judge. They will have to explain to a judge why they are making this application. However, if you apply for this then the court may decide to apply this to you too. Don't be afraid of this, many of the women who have these have told me that, in hindsight, they feel they're a good thing. Of course, please take your own legal advice and make sure any decision you make is the right one for you.

Oh, and don't be surprised if the ex-partner who is abusing you through the courts then gets really angry when you start any form of counter action. It is very common for the anger to escalate once you fight back. Document everything, communicate only in writing and as minimally as you can. A good rule of thumb is to read any communication out in the voice of a TV crime drama lawyer where they are trying to make you sound as bad as possible, before you send it. Then sleep on it. Then read it again and send it if it passes these two litmus tests.

Abuse and Class

I don't know how to say this without it sounding awful. I don't mean it that way. I just never thought I would be classed as an abused woman. I live in a thatched cottage, my children go to boarding school, I have a trust fund for goodness sake! I'd give the queen a run for her money in the poshness stakes. I mean, I actually enjoy going to the polo! And here I am admitting it happened to me. I didn't even see it for years. He wasn't hugely physically abusive. He pushed me a couple of times. He threatened to slap me when he was drunk. He used to pinch me a lot, in places where other people couldn't see the tiny little bruises. The main problem was the silence. If ever I challenged him about anything, he would sulk and then not speak to me. His record was three weeks. Imagine! Three weeks of silence. He would ridicule me in public too. He once measured my waist in front of our friends at a dinner party. He couldn't stop laughing about it at the time; he wanted to show how much weight I'd put on since we met as teenagers.

No one else was laughing but he didn't seem to care. Even worse was that I laughed too. It was the only way to get through those kind of evenings. Jane, 45.

Abuse knows no limits. You can be a millionaire and be abused in a relationship. You can be royalty and be abused in a relationship. Likewise, you can be on the breadline and yet be in the most loving and equal partnership. Money and class are no shield from abuse and whether you elongate your vowels and live in a castle or shorten them and live in a bedsit, you do not deserve it. Not all abuse leaves bruises and it's never acceptable.

Chapter 7

Narcissism

What is Narcissistic Personality Disorder? (NPD)

My mum was involved in a car accident. I rushed to the hospital to find her in a really bad way. I'd called my husband on the way to ask him to get there as soon as he could, as it was looking like she might not make it. It took him two hours and, by that point, I was being asked about organ donation. He arrived with wet hair and smelling of aftershave. He had prioritised having a shower and ironing a shirt over coming to support me. He was always obsessed with how he looked but I just couldn't believe he would prioritise himself when my mum was about to die. Later on, I found a receipt for the drive-through car wash in our car. He'd done that on the way too and stopped for a coffee! His image was always more important than anything else. He treated the hospital staff with more kindness and charm than he did his own wife. I decided there and then that I wouldn't tolerate this bullshit anymore. My boyfriend now is so incredibly emotionally switched on, he drops everything if I need support and vice versa. It still shocks me. Selina, 39.

You'd be forgiven for feeling the word 'narcissism' is overused at the moment. It feels like the buzz term of the last few years. So, what is Narcissistic Personality Disorder (NPD)? The best way to describe it is as a person obsessed with the way other people see them, crucially not someone who is in love with themselves. If anything, they hate themselves.

Narcissists are believed to be made in childhood, traumatised in some way to feel that at their core they are worthless and unworthy of love. It isn't the case that if you experienced trauma as a child, you will definitely be a narcissist though.

The narcissist, because of the trauma (often emotional abandonment) they experienced as a child, believes themself to be unlovable, and they feel shame because of this. So, in order to hide this and make themselves feel safe, they construct their ideal of the perfect person who is worthy of love, and then act it out. There is no authenticity of self, just an act. And they must keep this act up and control anyone who is part of the act to ensure they don't relive the trauma of their childhood. They are obsessed with the projected fantasy image they have constructed for themselves which is usually grandiose.

And to protect this image, they will do anything. So, they may have constructed themselves as kind and thoughtful and compassionate. Then a peep of their true self will creep out; they might lose their temper with someone, for example. They will need to deny this happened in order to maintain the persona they have constructed. Lying is how the narcissist manages to cope with the duality of pretending to be a person they are not. If you call them out on any of their lies, you will be on the receiving end of narcissistic rage (see page 156), often including blame. They will do anything to make sure their cover isn't blown and to restore the vision of themselves in the persona they created. This can include using other people to discredit the person who has caught them out, taking legal action and weaponising children.

There's not much to like about narcissists once the curtain falls and you see them for what they are. If you can take a positive from having been in a relationship with one, remember they only attach themselves to people who they feel offer them something; money, power, good looks (social currency), lifestyle etc. They also tend to target people who are caring, empathetic and avoidant of conflict. Oh, and they will often find you when you are at a vulnerable point in your life; heartbroken from a relationship ending, bereaved, just moved to a new area, having a professional crisis. There's something of the vulture about them.

It's worth noting that we all have a degree of narcissism (not NPD). At one end of the spectrum narcissism is part of a healthy ego function where you have a level of confidence, drive, can speak up for yourself and are able to ensure your needs are met. Narcissistic traits can serve us; at times putting our needs and desires first. It's your emotional response to acting in a selfish way that is indicative. For example, a person who behaves with a lack of empathy and then feels remorse for it later would be described as not having strong narcissistic qualities. Narcissistic traits do not equal narcissistic personality disorder (NPD). You'll notice though, for ease, I have referred to a person with NPD (diagnosed or undiagnosed) as a 'narcissist' in this chapter.

How to Spot a Narcissist

During the divorce, his narcissism ramped up a level. He actually put in one of his emails (clearly drafted by him and sent by his solicitor, he gave the game away by using deliberately grand words, one of his habits), that I should not be pursuing 50% of the assets as my dad was in receipt of a good pension and would easily be able to give me some of his money each month.

Seriously! The entitlement of him to think my dad's hard-earned teacher's pension was his to claim and dish out to other people. I look back now and realise I ignored a lot of his NPD traits. He was a total fantasist, even made me go and look at houses with swimming pools and tennis courts when we had a budget for a three-bed semi. He is now with a much younger woman who is lapping up his nonsense. I really hope she gets out before she has babies with him. Jacey, 37.

I've listed the key traits of a person with NPD but remember that just because your narcissist doesn't display all of them, doesn't mean they don't have it. Traits present to a greater or lesser extent in each narcissist.

1. A grandiose sense of self

We're not just talking vanity or arrogance here. We're not talking someone knowing they are talented and not being afraid to say so. Grandiosity is an unrealistic sense of superiority and, boy, does the narcissist suffer from it. It's not rooted in them actually believing, deep down, that they are better than others (quite the opposite – see What is Narcissistic Personality Disorder?, page 136). It presents in the narcissist displaying to the outside world the belief they are special, unique and too good for an ordinary life or regular people. They'll attach themselves to those with a high status, hang out in grand places and peacock about with ostentatious displays of wealth in belongings. So, if you're targeted by the narcissist, it's because they think you are worth something in social currency. Image is all and they will do anything to maintain others thinking they are special, including lying, exaggerating and often taking glory for things they've had little or no part in. Think of them as being the leading actor in their own screenplay, having chosen everyone around them to support their role best. You're a bit part.

2. Living in a fantasy world

The sad thing is for someone with NPD that their skill set rarely supports their grandiose view of themselves, so they have to construct a make-believe fantasy world to kid others and, importantly, themselves. To do this they have to lie about success, power, sex appeal…everything. This extends to all areas of their lives; exam results, their family background, where they live, their job title, their shoe size, height, salary, anything and everything will be twisted, fabricated and manipulated to ensure the world they live in is suitable for a quite brilliant person, i.e, them. As we all know, the problem with lies is that a lie begats a lie and so on until it's exhausting trying to maintain this alternative reality. The problems start when someone starts to unpick the lies, which is often the person closest to the narcissist (you?). By noticing that their eyes are grey and not green, or asking them what it was like to study at Balliol College, Oxford, when it turns out they went to Oxford Brookes, you are tugging at, and ultimately pulling down, the fantasy walls, and for daring to do this, even if with innocent intentions, you will experience extreme anger (see Narcissistic Rage, page 156) from them. Once you start to poke holes in their stories, a narcissist's feelings of intense shame and self-loathing are stoked. It's not uncommon for narcissist's partners to become complicit in their lies, if only to keep the peace.

3. Seeking praise and respect

For the narcissist to maintain their feeling of superiority, they need a supply of praise and respect from others. They know deep down they're no better than anyone else, they suspect they're actually an awful human being, so they don't have a way to buoy their own sense of self internally. This is where the people who the narcissist has chosen to surround themselves with come in. The narcissist will seek a constant stream of admiration, praise and attention. You will often find they embed themselves into community roles to gain this; scouting, the church, charities, governor roles, at the expense of contributing properly in their own homes. Community praise is a heady fix for the narcissist, as it comes from multiple streams of respect and praise, some of it discussed without their presence ('isn't Graham amazing for everything he does for the homeless shelter, you know he even spent his own birthday working there?') so that the praise becomes a runaway train that needs less attendance and feeding than their primary supply givers of attention need. This is catnip to the narcissist, as they receive maximum adoration for minimum effort.

4. Having a sense of entitlement

For the narcissist to keep up the belief (to themselves and others) that they are special and superior, they will display a sense of entitlement in regard to money, status, affection, sex, etc. to support this world view. Interestingly, if you mirror this back to the narcissist, they will almost always say you are selfish and retaliate with stone walling (silent treatment), anger or outrage at your audacity. Child maintenance is a classic area where this sense of entitlement rears its head. Often the narcissist will be disgusted that you expect them to pay towards the upkeep of the children and will do everything in their power to minimise this cost liability, however they will absolutely think nothing of booking an expensive holiday at the same time. Because they deserve a holiday, nay, they are entitled to a holiday. For you to try to access this money to pay towards the children is selfish of you. It's no coincidence that when faced with having to co-parent with a narcissist, it's common to feel you are losing your mind.

5. Having no empathy

The narcissist is so obsessed with themselves and maintaining the façade they've constructed, they lack the ability to feel empathy for others. Remember that other people are bit parts in the fantasy fairy tale of their life; supporting roles to their lead. This can be purposeful ('of course I took the praise for the merger being so lucrative, it was my idea, not my boss's, anyway, he doesn't need the money and I deserve it'), but often it is just a behaviour they display without malicious intent. It's second nature and, I think, a defence mechanism. If they let themselves think deeply about how their behaviour impacts on others, their whole world would come crumbling down. It's all part of the illusion they've created.

6. Being a bully

The narcissist's sense of self is very weak; after all, it's a construction. So, if the narcissist feels that someone else is a threat to them, whether they're more talented, intelligent, popular, confident, or perhaps if they challenge them or refuse to pander to them, they will seek to pull them down. This might be through sarcasm, blaming, negging, patronising, insulting, bullying and even name-calling and threats.

This makes the narcissist sound like someone with zero redeeming qualities, which begs the question of why you might have gotten involved with one, but they will often be extremely charming alongside these traits. They're masters of love bombing (see page 143) and will expertly reel people in. You're not stupid for having been duped by one.

The Cycle

It felt like a romantic movie that slowly turned into a psychological thriller and then into a horror film. He was SO nice to me when we met, said he had never felt this connection. The sex was mind-blowing, he made me feel like a princess. Then he started to say little things that'd make me feel crap about myself. If I ever asked him not to be unkind, he'd deny he said anything, so then I thought I was going mad. I even went to the GP and had an early onset dementia test as I was worried about my memory. When he left it was brutal. He refused to give me his new address, said he didn't want to know anything about our son and that he would only see him when he had the time, on an ad hoc basis. I packaged up half of our wedding photos for him and he put them in the bin outside my house. It was incredibly painful to go from being held up in such high regard to being treated like the shit on his shoe. Becca, 35.

There's a cyclical nature to a relationship with a narcissist. They can be divided into three key stages:

1. Idealise

Also called the love bombing phase (see page 143). This feels intoxicating as you're placed on a very high pedestal by the narcissist. They will accelerate the relationship, bombard you will verbal and physical displays of affection and make you believe you are so similar that you're soulmates. There's usually a lot of gifts, sex, compliments and grand gestures such as moving in together within days, fast proposals, or suggestions of trying for a baby. This phase lasts for weeks, sometimes months but rarely longer than a year. Common phrases the narcissist will use during this phase would not be out of place in a romantic film:

'I've never felt like this before.'
'You're my soulmate.'
'You're not like the other women I've dated.'
'I feel like I've known you all my life.'
'You're the woman I want to have my children with.'
'I don't see the point in hanging out with my friends now I've met you.'

2. Devalue

The narcissist now has you under their spell. You're feeling high from their attention, think you've finally met the man you'll grow old with. You're hooked. At this point the chase has begun to wind down for the narcissist. They have you. There's nothing left to pursue, which is disappointing for them. There's also the concern, now you're close, that you'll start to see that they're not the person they've been saying they are, that this is all an act. To keep you in check they subtly begin to put you down, withdraw sex, stop hugging and showing affection, disappear for periods of time with no explanation, flirt with others and/or gaslight you (see page 148). During this devaluing phase the narcissist won't be unpleasant all the time, they'll mix it up a bit. They know if they treat you too badly, you'll scarper before the next 'supply' (usually the romantic partner to follow you) has been identified. So, they'll be kind, then nasty, and so on, until you start to doubt your sanity. Throughout this phase, the narcissist will likely say things to destabilise you and make you blame yourself, including normalising their abusive behaviour:

'You're being oversensitive.'
'My mum doesn't like you but I always defend you to her.'
'You're so like my ex.'
'You're being really jealous and insecure and you know how unattractive I find that.'
'I shouldn't be made to feel bad for staying out all night, you need to learn to trust.'
'If you accuse me of cheating then maybe I will cheat, may as well.'

3. Discard

If you can visualise yourself as a cup that's been consumed by the narcissist, the discard phase occurs when they've drained you. You're empty, you have nothing left to give, so they don't have any use for you. The very thing they were attracted to, the qualities you had which gave them social currency, have been depleted and now you don't have the same worth to them. It's sad really that the narcissist will always destroy the qualities they were originally interested in. Once the source of supply is dry, they're off to find a new one. It's not uncommon for this discard phase to happen alongside the narcissist securing a new supply. As this new relationship shores up, they will disentangle from the first relationship but will importantly need to leave the primary relationship as the victor. They will communicate this to you and probably others too:

'You won't find anyone else as good as me.'
'You only have yourself to blame.'
'You let yourself go, what did you expect?
'You're not as exciting as you were when we met.'
'I had to leave her, she wasn't stable.'

'I stayed for a long time, but, in the end, I couldn't be with someone as depressing as her.'

It can be hard to see these phases when you're in them. If you're reading this and are not sure if this cycle was part of your relationship, speak to a trusted friend and ask if they can identify any of the markers for you. It can be difficult to see what's right in front of you when the experience is traumatic.

Love Bombing

By the time I met him I'd dated a lot of men, I thought I knew every trick in the book, but with him it was breath-taking. He blew me away. One minute we were on a pretty average date, we said goodbye and I was left thinking that he was nice and seemed quite similar to me, but, honestly, I wouldn't rush to see him again. The next thing, flowers arrived at my work. Then he booked tickets to see a comedian I had said I liked in passing. Next thing he'd arranged a picnic in Green Park with every one of my favourite foods, and pink champagne. He just bombarded me with really touching gestures. And he increasingly seemed like the male version of me. We liked the same music, same food, had the same politics, values and aims in life. He started to talk about what our kids would be like, names even. I was utterly bowled over by him and even said to a friend at the time that I loved Fhim so much it felt like the love would destroy me – how right I was! There was a nagging sensation in the back of my mind that this all seemed too good to be true. He'd been a bit rude to one of my flatmates on a night out, and when I pulled him up on it, he said he was really stressed at work and basically made me feel sorry for him. He was a bit like Teflon in that respect. Four weeks after we met, he proposed and I said yes. A year later I sat in our house with a newborn baby in my arms and felt this sinking feeling that I'd been had. He wasn't at all like he seemed at first, he was actually pretty controlling and could be quite mean. (Just like he'd been to my flatmate, who declined the invitation to our wedding.) After our son was born, he brought clothes to the hospital for me to leave in and chose my smallest jeans and a tiny tight T shirt. I couldn't fit into them and he smirked as I tried. I wasn't sure I even liked him, let alone loved him. I told my mum I was worried he wasn't what he seemed and she just told me I'd made my bed and had to lie in it. It was only when our little boy was about three that I read an article in the paper about love bombing and realised this was exactly what had happened to me. I felt so sad as I was stuck in a marriage I didn't feel was real. And I'd brought another human into this. I decided to just get on with it. A decade and four kids later, I couldn't do it anymore, I left him. He was so shocked, I don't think he'll ever forgive me for leaving him, but I'll never forgive him for hoodwinking me. Tisha, 46.

So what's love bombing? Simply, it's where one person showers another with over the top gestures, gifts, affection and attention in order to gain control of them, and it's almost always a short phase at the beginning of a relationship. (Though can be revisited post relationship breakdown to exert control as a manipulation technique. Ask yourself, if your ex-narcissist is suddenly nice to you, kind even, what do they want?)

The love bomber often mirrors the other person to make them feel that they're soulmates and once they 'have' them, then the subtle putdowns start (see The Cycle, page 140). This mirroring is powerful stuff as our pleasure receptors light up when opinions are echoed. Is it conscious behaviour? The jury's out on that.

Love bombing comes in many guises, but there are five main broad areas:

1. Gifts

Spending a lot of money on a gift that's really over the top is a classic first sign of love bombing. Plane tickets for a weekend in Rome for example, leaving in two days, without checking you're free. You feel you can't say no given how much money has been committed, but actually they didn't check you had plans, and you did. But it's such a lovely thing to have organised that you go anyway. Though they do mention how much it cost quite a lot when you're there. And you feel like you're lucky and a bit indebted to them all weekend.

2. Contact

Love bombing feels like an onslaught. Constant text messages, phone calls and emails saying you are perfect, they have never loved anyone like they love you, you're their ideal woman. You're giddy with the compliments, but also you're high up on a pedestal and guess which is the only way down? The sheer volume of messages and calls feels overwhelming, but you feel you must reply. It's not polite to just read them. They have read receipt on their emails anyway so they'd know. You feel a bit watched and monitored by all the communication.

3. Attention

They'll demand your undivided attention, often making you go missing in action to the other significant people in your life. You'll justify missing your best friend's birthday bash to go to an amazing new restaurant they've booked because they went to a lot of effort to get the reservation and you don't want to disappoint them, plus they seemed so hurt when you mentioned you really ought to go to Andrea's birthday. You realise that being in a relationship with them is a full-time job. You're leaving work slightly early to meet them outside their office because they say they like to see your beautiful face as soon as they finish for the night. You're not seeing the people who are important to you as much as you'd like to and are starting to feel a bit isolated.

4. Romanticising

Love bombing feels like a Hollywood film at times. They'll say your love was written in the stars, soulmates, destined to be together, that even if you hadn't met on the night you did, you'd have met somehow, somewhere, it was meant to be! Fate! They create mythology around your meeting so that if you think about getting out, you feel like you're going against the order of the world. To leave is to turn the sun and the moon on their head, it's not the natural order of things.

5. Boundary pushing

Love bombing pushes boundaries that will make you feel uncomfortable. A fast proposal, a suggestion of moving in together when you don't even know how they take their tea yet, discussion of trying for a baby before you've met their parents. And if you try to pull back a bit and take things slowly, they'll be pretty upset. Are you daring to suggest that this special love you share will follow a mere mortal's timelines? Your love is different, remember (see point 4).

Surely being really into someone and being love bombed is just a symptom of falling in love, right? The honeymoon phase. Nope. Wrong. It's a form of manipulation and it's as intoxicating as it is effective. If the amount of attention, gifts and boundary pushing gave you an uneasy feeling in the early days and was then followed by a very different version of the suitor, chances are you've been love bombed.

Don't feel stupid for falling foul of a love bomber. It's easily done. We all want to be loved, don't we? And we've been conditioned by Hollywood films to think that grand love gestures are the best gestures. I've been love bombed more than once; I think it's down to my people pleasing nature, something lots of women suffer from. Every time it's happened to me my body has tried to alert me to it physically. I have not had many panic attacks in my life, but they have always been in response to an almost animal bodily rejection of the sensation of love bombing. I have finally learnt to listen to my body at the age of 41.

Also, I was raised not to be rude, like a 'good girl' (as so many of us women are), so when someone is really kind and generous, I feel I ought to show how grateful I am. You can't change the past, but you can remain vigilant to love bombing so that it doesn't happen to you again. Since I divorced, if a man moves too fast, buys me expensive things and tries to isolate me, I run for the hills.

Oh, and as a final note on love bombing, it's used by cult leaders to control their followers and ensure they do exactly as they are told, including atrocities such as murder and/or suicide. It is powerful and dangerous.

Breadcrumbing

I was chatting to my best girlfriend and saying how I was so pleased that after years of hell with my ex-husband, he had sent an email where instead of saying 'Sara' at the beginning of his email he put 'Dear Sara'. I was banging on about how this was such a good sign and meant we might be able to be friendly in the future, and she stopped me and said 'when did the bar get so low for you?' and I realised he was reeling me back in with the use of 'dear'. I was that used to receiving unpleasant emails and texts that this made me feel hopeful and excited. Sara, 48.

You have to watch out for this, because throwing out these very tiny glimmers of hope (throwing breadcrumbs to you, hence the term 'breadcrumbing') is a classic narcissistic tactic to keep you under their control. You'll notice these little positive interactions will often occur just as you are finally done with them. They're throwing you crumbs to keep you interested because they need you and the attention you bring, not because they care about you. All interactions are done with self-interest and to prove to themselves that they are still entitled to your attention, do remember that.

One of the best gifts you can give yourself if you feel the relationship with the narcissist is still up and down post separation/divorce, is to keep a diary. It doesn't have to be long entries, just short details of daily interactions, whether they were initiated by you or him, and whether they are positive or negative. Try colour coding them and use a system of dots – green for you, red for him, one dot is least positive, five dots most positive. You'll start to see a pattern whereby when the green dots are non-existent or very low, what will follow are red dots in plentiful supply. It's a push-me–pull-you dance, and, for your own sanity, when you see it on a page in red and green, you need to make an effort to put a stop to it. (See Grey Rock, page 152.)

Hoovering

It's like clockwork, just when I think I am feeling stronger and have put him behind me, he gets in contact for some spurious reason. So far we've had the anniversary of my brother's death (who he never met!), my birthday, a dream he had where I left the country, and even huge baskets of fruit sent to my work after the kids told him I'd had a cold. I just want to be left alone. I'm still stupid enough to think for a split second it might be a sign he's changed, but I soon come to my senses. Dana, 45.

Hoovering is a form of manipulation used by someone with NPD to suck you back in. This isn't breadcrumbing, which is much more about keeping you at arm's length, but compliant. Hoovering is emotionally charged, whether direct or indirect. It can be an apology for their previous behaviour and a promise they've changed for the better. It might be a text on an anniversary or birthday to show they still remember important dates. It might be an email saying they have been dreaming about you. It can often take the form of using drama or trauma to re-establish contact – perhaps their mum has died and they want to talk. It could be gifts that they know hold meaning to you. It can be message-passing through third parties such as your children or parents ('Mummy will always be my one true love.'). They might try to start an argument with you about something you had stopped ruminating about years ago. They might even threaten to self-harm or kill themself if you don't agree to talk to them and consider their pleas that they've changed.

Don't be fooled. The reason the narcissist is behaving like this is because they see you as a bit part in the play of their life. You're there to serve them. So if they're feeling low, lonely or in need of validation, they may try to re-establish contact to serve this need. If you bite and agree to the contact, the narcissist sees this as a win and has gained some new supply from you because you've shown you're still capable of their manipulation.

Don't engage with hoovering. If you can go completely no contact with a narcissist then that's the best way forward. For those who share the care of their children with the narcissist low contact and the grey rock (page 152) technique are useful. And if you think that your ex may genuinely harm themselves, report their threat to the police and request a welfare check. You are not responsible for your ex anymore.

Gaslighting

We'd just moved into a new house and the radiators were on full blast. It was July and like a sauna, so I called him at work and asked him if he could explain to me how to turn them off. I'd already tried everything I could think of. He told me, confidently, that radiators are always on and can't be turned off and that I needed to open a window to cool the house. I knew this was complete nonsense but the degree of his gaslighting was so strong, I did what he said. Later on, he came home and asked why all the windows were open and when I reminded him of what he'd said he denied it. Nina, 59.

Strange name, isn't it? It comes from a 1930s play called *Gaslight* (made into a film starring Ingrid Bergman in 1944) where a husband convinces his wife that she's hallucinating and mentally ill by denying that their gas-fuelled lights are dimming, despite being responsible for it.

Gaslighting is a form of psychological abuse which often develops gradually (akin to the boiling frog effect) where a person makes their victim question their sanity, memories and/or perception of reality. Here are a few examples of gaslighting:

'Why are you all dressed up? Our dinner date is tomorrow night, not tonight. You must have written it down wrong.'

'Your labour really wasn't that bad, I don't think you're remembering it properly.'

'Thanks for the aftershave but I really don't like that particular one, I definitely said not to buy that one. I didn't say to buy it, silly, you're confused!'

'I don't know what you're talking about. I think you're trying to confuse me.'

'I was joking, you're overreacting.'

'I wasn't flirting with the girl at the bar. You completely imagined it. I would never put my hand on a stranger's back or touch their hair.'

'So your mum thinks she saw me with another woman? Wow, another crazy thing she made up to split us up and you believe it.'

'You're very tired at the moment so it's not surprising that you are imagining things. Maybe we need to book an appointment at the doctor's for you.'

'You said I could use the holiday money to get a new bike, don't you remember?'

Being gaslit is a form of control, a way to ensure the gaslighter is in charge of the relationship. The person on the receiving end feels stupid, incompetent, hopeless and confused. They doubt themselves, apologise and feel they are losing their grip on reality. They might seek antidepressants or anti-anxiety medication. They may actually become anxious and depressed as a result of the gaslighting. It's a subtle but powerful form of abuse.

Gaslighting doesn't end because a marriage does, it can continue throughout and post the divorce. One the most helpful things you can do for yourself is to write down what's happening in a diary. Sorting the truth from the distortion presented by the gaslighter will give you some power back. Then make the effort to disengage from the gaslighter using the grey rock technique (page 152) and remind yourself that you will not be able to change the narcissist, so don't try to. Minimal contact and engagement are key to healing.

Flying Monkeys

After we split, I thought it was all over, I was excited about my future, about moving on, but the nastiness continued through other people. People who I thought were my friends ended up telling him how I was coping, my own sister even told him really private stuff. I felt utterly betrayed by her. I think her betrayal was far worse than anything he did. Roz, 38.

The term 'flying monkeys' is used to describe the people the narcissist uses to carry out psychological and/or emotional abuse on their behalf. They're deployed to gather intelligence to use against you, destroy your reputation and deposit titbits of information with you to cause distress. The term is borrowed from the film *The Wizard of Oz* where the Wicked Witch uses flying monkeys to terrorise; importantly, they never speak or act independently.

No one is off-limits for flying monkey recruitment; friends, colleagues, family (yours and his), children, counsellors, faith leaders. They gather information, pass messages, assassinate your character publicly and act as a protector of sorts to the narcissist, often completely unaware they're being manipulated. Vulnerable themselves and easily bullied, their loyal following feeds the narcissist's supply. Their service proves something very important to the narcissist; that they are more popular than you and are 'winning' in the battle of your separation/divorce. Some flying monkeys are aware of their role, but, even when this is so, there's always a degree of manipulation at play.

Flying monkeys are used as a punishment technique. The narcissist can't be seen to behave in an overtly abusive manner by others as that would pull down the fantasy world they have constructed, so they use others to do this. There's usually a covert element to this; for example, they may tell one of their monkeys about a time you lied about something and suggest this proves you are untrustworthy. They'll remove crucial details which might explain why you did this. The seeds of doubt are sown that you're a liar, so if you unwittingly confide in a monkey that your ex is lying about something, they will question this, pass it on and gossip about it. You're the liar, after all.

Flying monkeys can be those you least expect. The narcissist will target those whose allegiance with them will cause you the most distress, and prove their innocence and inherent goodness the most, so don't be surprised if they target your mother, sister or best friend. Consequently, your ability to trust is hugely damaged. Trying to mend relationships with those close to you who have acted as their flying monkeys is a long process.

If you've split from a narcissist don't wait for the flying monkeys to appear, pre-empt their arrival. Lock down all your social media by changing the permissions for anyone who you suspect is vulnerable to your ex's manipulation. On Facebook this involves going to your profile and ensuring it's private and also going through your friends list, clicking 'edit' before choosing the level of information they can access. Better still, when going through a high-combat divorce and separation with a narcissist, disable all social media for the time being. Offline, be careful who you confide in and if you do need to vent, consider professional one-on-one counselling where you can be sure that everything you say is confidential.

If the flying monkeys do arrive, you need to disengage, which is admittedly hard; after all, it's human nature to defend ourselves. But, arguing with a flying monkey is akin to arguing with a narcissist; what you say will be twisted to fit the narrative which they're looking to support. Cut off their supply, so if they start to engage you in any conversation about your ex, the divorce, or anything contentious, change the subject. Stick to subjects which are dull beyond dull. Weather is a good one. Or direct the conversation back onto them, ask them what they've been up to, how they are, etc. But don't give anything away.

Oh, and especially beware the new partner of the narcissist who wants to be friends with you. The narcissist does NOT want you to develop a friendship with their new partner, so if this is initiated, they must feel the new partner is sufficiently under their spell of control that they can risk the two of you interacting. Be polite but ultimately avoid and do not share any information. Being busy is always a good excuse.

<u>Supply</u>

He left me like an empty shell. He took everything he could from me, literally and emotionally. Thousands of pounds spent on his various hare-brained schemes to get rich quick, but, even worse, my confidence was zapped, and at times my sanity too! Once he'd taken everything from me, he looked for a new supply and now I can see the same process happening to her. I stupidly tried to tell her and of course he used this as evidence that I am obsessed with him and told everyone I was trying to get him back. I really wasn't, I just didn't want her to go through what I did. His ex long-term girlfriend had tried to warn me when we first got together and I'd written her off as bitter, so I guess I can't blame his new victim for not taking me seriously. Cerys, 44.

Narcissists aren't able to rely on their interior world to form a sense of self, so they depend on other people to validate their existence. The narcissist surrounds themselves with people who form their supply, in the same way that an addict might see their stash of drugs/alcohol. The narcissist needs a supply of attention as a way of numbing the pain they feel (the suspicion they have, that deep down they are unlovable and worthless). Importantly the nature of the supply doesn't need to be positive, which is why it's common after divorcing a narcissist for them to continue to engage with you in a negative way (not paying child maintenance, dropping off children very late or early, not giving consent for medical treatment for children, starting legal action years after agreeing informal terms of a split etc.). The supply is all about the narcissist gaining attention, so that the self-constructed story of their worth can be embellished upon. For example, you needing to go to court to defend the narcissist trying to exit the marriage with all the assets is a good tale to spin to others that you are unable to let go and are trying to bleed them dry of everything they ever worked for. You're clearly obsessed with them and won't let them move on. It doesn't matter what the truth is. It's the whirlwind of power, control, attention and the potential of winning that the narcissist is using to numb their pain.

Understanding that any form of attention is a need for the narcissist will make it easier to ignore them when they're playing up and trying to elicit a negative response. It's tempting to try to put the narcissist right when they accuse you of all sorts, but that's what they want. So-called 'winning' with a narcissist invariably involves inaction. Ultimately, despite seeking control over others, a narcissist is weak and needs your supply of attention more than you need them. This supply of attention is like oxygen to a narcissist. When you fight a narcissist, you breathe life into them. So, don't do it.

Grey Rock

When he first left me for a woman YOUNG ENOUGH TO BE HIS DAUGHTER, I did everything to show him what he was missing. I lost a lot of weight (albeit not intentionally). I had a bit of 'help' in the facial area at a clinic. I bought new clothes and always looked relaxed and happy when he came to the house to pick the children up. I made a point of posting photos on Facebook of myself on nights out... I wanted to make him jealous, even though there was no way I wanted him back. In hindsight I think it made things worse, as his game playing escalated the more I tried to show him how great I was. A friend of mine told me about the grey rock technique and it really did work. I now hold my head up high that I don't seek or need his attention and it's working really well. He doesn't seem to be as bothered about punishing me over money and the children as he was when I was at the peak of my 'look how amazing I am' behaviour. Jo, 52.

Have you heard of this? I came to this a bit late, but I think it's a really good idea for anyone navigating a difficult break-up. It's essentially about cutting off the narcissist's supply. Grey rock is a technique where you make yourself as interesting and inert as a grey rock. Your main aim is to make the narcissistic ex lose interest in you and move on to others for their attention and drama hit. It's not an easy thing to do, though. You must not show any emotion to your ex, don't say anything interesting, don't tell them anything about your life. Don't share anything on social media which could be fed back to them by others. Importantly it's not about being rude or unpleasant, it's about being as dull as ditch water. Keep all replies factual and short. Don't look good for drop-offs with kids. Wear shapeless clothes. Look a bit tired. The less of a catch the narcissist sees you as, the less interested he will be in getting his supply from you, and the faster he will move onto his next victim.

Now, being a grey rock is slightly soul-destroying. It feels like yet another form of control, right? Surely the only way you can break free of your ex isn't to play games? Your feminist soul will be screaming that you really shouldn't have to behave in a particular way in order to be free of a man. But it works. Difficult to do, feels wrong, but it works. Reframe it as having the best poker face going. If you are easily provoked, you are easily controlled, so give nothing away. Try it, but don't tell him you're doing it.

Counter Parenting and Parallel Parenting

I feel like it's one step forwards and two steps back parenting with him. In fact, I'd go as far as to say it's moved onto damage limitation now. He says the most damaging things to the kids, then I deal with the fall-out. And the lack of safe care is a constant source of worry. He let our 12 year old take the three year old swimming alone on holiday! Luckily they were fine, but this kind of unsafe parenting (or lack of parenting) is another way to keep me under his control. He knows now that I will never relax when he takes the children away on holiday. I spend the time they are away drinking too much and worrying. Just the break I need, right?!' Yasmin, 36.

A narcissist is not capable of consistently co-parenting because it requires working as a team and putting another human (or humans) ahead of their own needs. If you have witnessed a narcissist co-parent effectively ask yourself if they are doing it consistently and without gleaning supply from it. (Are they using it to gain attention from others about how great they are at being divorced, how they are selfless?) You do not co-parent with a narcissist, at best you parallel parent, at worst you have to counter parent.

Okay, positive side first, if you have to parent alongside a narcissist, it will make you a far more attentive parent. You will always be in some form of competition (that you didn't agree to enter into, admittedly) with the parent with NPD, so you will have to keep your slate spotless. You'll need to think before you act and will probably be kinder, more empathetic and genuinely parent to a higher standard.

Parallel parenting is the best-case scenario for having to parent alongside a narcissist. This is where you limit your interactions with them (by using a specially designed app such as My Family Wizard to communicate, a Parent Communication Book passed between houses used for factual essential information, or agreeing contact and other important details through a legally binding document called a Child Arrangements Order (see page 100)). Parallel parenting relies on having enough detail agreed to be able to disengage from each other, allowing each parent to get on with their relationship with the children, when they are in their care.

In reality, a narcissist will initially parallel parent within the parameters (their supply being that they are *having* to use this method to calm the situation between you; they will enjoy a lot of attention through telling everyone and anyone about this), but once it proves to be working, they will ramp up their behaviour to gain more (negative) supply. Perhaps in a minor way such as not ensuring the children do their homework, or in a major way through neglect. The aim is to re-engage you, to provoke a response and thus gain supply through drama. If your ex is neglecting the children, of course you have to protect them; see the chapter on children (page 79) for more details on how you can do this. If they are trying to re-engage you through minor displays of crappy parenting, you will need to counter parent.

Counter parenting is about minimising any negativity for your children inflicted by the narcissist and actively trying to undo damage. It's an all-encompassing task that requires a lot of time and energy. You'll need respite from how tiring it is to counter parent; frequent periods of time alone to recharge. The key to trying to counteract damage done by a narcissist is being the opposite of them. You are kind, empathetic and loving. You listen to them, allow them to be themselves, don't put any boundaries on how they receive love and care. You are attentive to their unique needs. There is nothing transactional about your love; it is infinite and unconditional.

Here are some practical ideas for counter parenting:

1. Be clear and firm with boundaries. One of the key traits of a narcissist is to move goalposts to cause confusion, or to change them to love bomb. Be the safe, consistent, predictable and clear parent. And 'parent' is the key word here. Not friend, not 'just like a sister', please no. Your own friends are your emotional support, not your child. If your ex is being a pain, don't vent to your child. Hold your tongue. They could be hearing all manner of bitchiness about you from the narcissist, don't add to this. Model good behaviour.

2. Limit contact with the narcissist parent. Don't reply straight away and remember sometimes you don't need to reply at all if there's no requirement. Agree the method of contact and stick to it. If your ex sends emails littered with personal venomous attacks, do not counterattack. Draft a response if it's required and then sleep on it, be unemotional and brief. (See Grey Rock, page 152).

3. Communicate clearly and regularly. The narcissist is a truth-twister, make sure you're not. Listen to your children, be present when in their company (not distracted by the latest email nonsense from the narcissist infiltrating your phone), admit when you've made mistakes and apologise if you messed up. If this isn't part of how you parent at the moment, you may want to formalise it by having a regular family meeting where each person gets to bring up subjects dear to them. There are a lot of online resources available on how to hold productive family meetings.

4. Warmly encourage individuality in your children. The narcissist manipulates the people around them to fit their own narrative, so as your children get older, their need to develop individual identities may be quashed by the narcissist if their interests and personality don't provide bragging rights. Having *one* parent who sees their child as unique and supports their hopes and dreams is a magnificent gift.

5. Don't express pity to your child, verbally or covertly. This goes for pity towards them having one narcissist parent and also pity towards yourself. Why? It perpetuates a victim mentality. We've all met adults like this and life is hard for them. Everything is a trial because that is their narrative. This doesn't mean you should be aggressively positive about everything. Far from it. Being able to sit with another person's feelings without trying to cheer them, make them look on the bright side or show pity, is an important parenting (and life) skill.

6. It's highly unlikely you will be able to influence a narcissist parent, much less intervene, when your children are in their care. When your child tells you they are unhappy with some of the questionable things the narcissist is saying or doing, your instinct as a parent is to protect them. Unless you suspect there is inadequate care/abuse, the best course of action is to help your child empower themselves when in the care of the narcissist. For younger children, play-centred therapy can be a really useful way to coach them with these skills. When it comes to older children, narcissists are often the making of their own demise. Teenagers are masters of calling out inconsistency, inadequacy and injustice.

7. Arrange respite for yourself. It may be not to everyone's taste, but yoga and meditation can help to calm and centre your thoughts. Or running, or perhaps gardening. Whatever it is, find something that allows you to calm your mind and deal with the anxiety and stress caused by counter parenting. You will need it to regulate your emotions. If your own stress and anxiety spills out into your everyday interactions, it can become a part of your parenting style. Anxious parents often create anxious children and that's not a gift you want to give your children if at all possible. And remember, there will come a point where this will be behind you.

Narcissistic Rage

He used to lie over the most random things. I asked him to pick up some Easter eggs for the children I tutor and when he came back, he'd bought other things, but the eggs were missing. He told me a really long story about how the shop had said they weren't stocking them this year. I said it didn't matter if he'd forgotten, but that I'd seen them in the shop window when I drove past the day before and he went beetroot. He didn't speak to me for over a week after that little episode. Frieda, 29.

Narcissistic rage can be an intense and often terrifying outburst of anger, but it can also come in the form of silent treatment, passive aggressive avoidance or completely cutting someone out. It tends to happen when there's injury to their self-esteem, confidence or self-worth. People with NPD, despite displaying a high opinion of themselves, are very insecure in their sense of self, so criticisms or blows to their fragile ego will be met viciously. If one person works out that they aren't capable of something or that they have been lying, perhaps everyone will be onto them and the fraud will be exposed. If someone gets wise, a narcissist needs to shut them down as soon as possible.

Triangulation

He met someone new within about a fortnight of me asking him to leave, which was fine by me. I was glad he had a new focus, to be honest. Almost immediately he started to play us off against each other. I tried to talk to him about a problem between her daughter and ours, really calmly, and the next thing I knew she had banned me from picking our daughter up from her house. God knows what he'd told her. I knew what he was up to as he had done the same thing with a work colleague when we were together. I don't think he wanted his two worlds to collide in case his new girlfriend worked out he was a charlatan. Mia, 27.

If your ex has NPD and gets a new partner, don't be surprised if they start to play you off against each other. Especially if either of you show an interest in being friendly and getting along. This is a very bad thing for a person with NPD as they are worried their lies will catch up with them and they'll be exposed. It's common for a narcissist to play old and new partners off against each other to the degree whereby they will never be friends and compare notes. This is the ideal scenario; it creates drama, jealousy, stress and ensures the curtain doesn't fall and expose the narcissist.

The proper name for this is 'triangulation'; where a person brings a third party into a relationship (not always a romantic one and not always knowingly). The aim is to create confusion, jealousy and sometimes

or sadness, how they support each other as a team. That's what we're looking for next time.

What to Expect When You Split with a Narcissist

He was vicious. He told everyone I had had an affair, that I had tried it on with his brother, and that I had alcohol issues! All untrue, and actually he had more than one affair, he made multiple passes at our female friends and he also drank to excess, but he was so charming and so respected in our community that everyone believed him. I moved in the end as I couldn't handle the results of his smear campaign. Even now, on the odd occasion we have to have contact, he is still playing the victim. Daphne, 54.

Don't expect an amicable and kind split when you leave someone with NPD. You will have wounded them deeply, so prepare for the worst and be surprised (and suspicious) if it's any better than that.

Their main concern will be to save face, so expect a smear campaign of lies, usually involving recruiting others (Flying Monkeys, see page 149) to abuse you and strengthen their story. They will likely goad you to provoke a response and thus prove that you were the problem all along, making them able to claim they're the victim. They'll usually accuse you of all the things that they actually did themselves, which is, of course, infuriating.

You will need to accept that you won't gain closure after splitting up with a narcissist. Part of gaining closure at the end of a relationship is both parties accepting a proportion of blame for what went wrong and taking learnings from their part in the breakdown. Someone with NPD will not be able to do this. They are blame merchants, attributing all their problems to other people.

Accepting this dynamic will not change and learning to morph feelings of anger and hurt into pity towards the narcissist will help you to heal. I am also a firm believer in the power of positive romantic experiences being key to healing from a relationship with a narcissist. Jumping back on the horse is restorative, but it must be a healthy horse.

Accusations are Confessions for Narcissists

I did a lot of research online and now realise I was married to a narcissist. He is textbook in his behaviour. I have been extremely sad about it, I feel that the love we had together was one-sided, I don't even think that he is capable of loving in a normal way. It's been a tough ride. But one thing that I think has been helpful is realising that narcissists are not hugely bright and tend to follow a lot of the same patterns. It's been really helpful to remember that accusations are almost always confessions for a narcissist. I didn't really accept this for ages, but, honestly, coming to terms with this truth has been life-changing. In the early days when we were still trying to financially settle, he would accuse me of hiding savings. Then he, later on, accused me of having affairs. Only last week he accused me of preferring to spend time with my friends rather than our daughters. Guess what – he hid over £140,000 during the course of the marriage (only uncovered through a forensic accountant), he had numerous affairs with other women and men (I've had Facebook messages from more than one jilted girl/boyfriend with photos of his texts confirming this) and he regularly cancels seeing our girls for 'work functions' except he then gets tagged on social media showing he's out with his mates getting drunk. I'm not perfect, of course, but I haven't done any of these things. Katy, 44.

Just so you know, at some point, if you speak out about any kind of narcissistic abuse, either to friends and family, or to the police, social services, courts, etc. then your ex will counter accuse. I know this sounds bananas. I know, I know. But they do this.

Like caged animals, they lash out, and often being fairly unimaginative, they accuse what they themselves are guilty of. This can at times start to pre-empt their own behaviour. What I mean by that is that they will accuse you of, say, not declaring all your earnings, then a few months down the line you will find out that in fact *they* have not been doing this, just so that they can underpay child maintenance. They may well accuse you of parental alienation just at the point when they are telling your beautiful children how mummy is evil and a slag and, if it weren't for mummy breaking up the family, then everyone would be happy and together still. Listen very carefully to what they accuse you of, as it can often inform you of their next move or, indeed, what they've already been up to.

Do I have Narcissistic Personality Disorder?

I've had some years now to reflect on how I behaved when I was married. I was definitely married to a man with undiagnosed NPD. He was textbook. But I now wonder if I was too. I have spent a lot of money on therapy trying to understand if I have the same condition but my therapist is adamant that isn't the case and said he has never in 35 years of practice had someone with NPD worry that they have it. The rule is, he said, if you have enough empathy and concern about your actions to think you have NPD, you definitely don't. Lauren, 48.

Due to the nature of NPD, (and let's remember, it's a pretty damning list of attributes whereby a person will be a fantasist, lie, have little or no empathy, a grandiose sense of self and feel entitled to what they desire), few people with it are able to recognise it in themselves. That doesn't mean they won't accuse others of being a narcissist.

Should I Tell Him?

After one especially awful email from him, I lost my temper and emailed him back saying he was a total narcissist monster. I had fantasies that he might research it and get help, change even. Ha ha! What a fool I was. It made no difference. Alex, 30.

Those who get into a relationship with a narcissist are usually empathetic, caring, optimistic, generally good eggs. Therefore it makes sense that they will often harbour fantasies of the narcissist changing, and how better to set them on this path than telling them their suspicions. Stop right there. No, just no. Do NOT tell the narcissist you suspect they have NPD; it is a waste of your time and energy. They don't care. They won't change and the only reason you are telling them is because you want them to change. Focus your efforts on your own healing, not theirs.

Why Me?

I have now had two relationships with men with NPD. It's like I don't see it. I wish I had a better radar in my relationships. At work I am intuitive, switched on and the first person to call bullshit (I am a police inspector) and yet in my personal life I have had to accept that my judgement is poor and I am vulnerable to manipulation. I think if a psychologist spent some time with me, they'd link it back to my own dad, who was very distant. Terri, 44.

Being the target of someone with NPD feels intensely personal. It's hard not to take such abuse (for that is what it is) personally when it tends to implode catastrophically at the end. There are definite character traits and life experiences that can make you more vulnerable to being preyed on by someone with NPD:

1. You enhance their social standing and credibility. You might be accomplished in your work, you might be well respected in your community, you may come from an established and esteemed family. Perhaps you have won awards or are famous, or you are extremely beautiful, kind and have the kind of charisma that draws people to you. Whatever it is, you have something the narcissist is jealous of, and, being unable to farm this quality for themselves, they attach themselves to you parasitically.

2. You have a history of being hurt, either in childhood or in adult relationships. This might be emotional neglect or outright abuse. If you have already been in a painful relationship, especially one where you have been criticised, you will be more vulnerable to accepting it again.

3. You are open to persuasion. You're a person who is receptive to questioning life, opinions and the status quo. You often listen to other people's opinions and intuition and have been known to take on other's views easily.

4. You're a trusting soul. You are generous of mind, body and/or money. You are prone to being idealistic and even romantic at times.

5. You've always had to work for love. In your past, often in childhood, you have had to earn love. It may have felt transactional; for example, love being conditional upon being quiet, good or achieving good exam results. If you have already had to graft for love and validation in your past, you'll be more susceptible to the validation someone with NPD will use as a carrot.

In short, if you're successful, trusting and somewhat wounded, you're a good supply for a narcissist...

Chapter 8

Moving On

The thing I am most upset about isn't that he had an affair, it isn't that we had to sell the house as part of the divorce, not even that his new wife is beautiful and very slim. No, the thing that bothers me most is that after we split, I spent eighteen months mourning the loss of the seven years we were married. I saw it as a waste of my precious life. I couldn't view it with balance, I was too 'in' the anger. Then I flipped to the opposite and missed him like hell, and definitely viewed the marriage as better than it was. Neither way was helpful. I am so proud to say that I now can see it as a period that taught me a lot, gave me my sons and happily that the lessons I learnt will be things that stand me in good stead for the next chapter of my life. It wasn't a waste of time, but it was often painful and sometimes good. I am excited for what comes next. Lillian, 39.

When you're in that post-divorce period of reflection, it's tempting to write off the marital years as a waste of time, especially if things ended in a tempestuous fashion and betrayal was a theme. I remember when I had been married for a few years, trying to recollect my time being single and having trouble recalling the person I'd been. I'd moulded so completely into my idea of a married person and a mother, I couldn't search for the woman who existed before in the recesses of my brain. She existed in photos, which became memories, but otherwise she was a stranger. I'd bump into old colleagues at weddings who hadn't seen me since I'd married and be surprised at them speaking to me in what felt like an alien manner. They were chatting to the pre-married me and were surprised at my quizzical expression. Similarly, I was searching for some old emails recently and found a few from the early years of my marriage. The tone of voice and even the content sounded so unlike the me of now, that at first I thought the emails were from a friend. They weren't. I'd written them. But I don't remember being that person.

People change is what I'm saying, and us humans are very clever at adapting. If you can accept your marriage as an Act, rather than a waste of time, it will help you. In a play each Act helps the characters move towards the grand finale, doesn't it? Each Act has purpose; it isn't there as a filler. A marriage, even if wholly unhappy, once left, will have moved you on to the next Act, so it isn't lost time. It was not a waste of your life. Being that reductive leads to feelings of desperation and it's frankly untrue. For most people there *will* have been happy times in their marriage, just as there were unhappy times, and though looking back with rose-tinted glasses is also not a good thing, having a balanced view is something that comes with time and is healthy. Either vision, of it all being perfect or it all being awful, halts your healing. One makes for yearning, one for anger, both emotions that stall us.

Change is hard though. Moving your life into the next Act requires growth and growing can be painful. We have to become something more than we were before, which can feel unpleasant, difficult and emotionally draining. If you can sit with these feelings, they are often the stage that happens before big personal development, before we move on to the next phase of our life. The next Act.

You learn so much about yourself in adversity. I've said it before and I'll happily say it again: some of the most warm, wonderful and remarkable people I know have experienced significant hardship whether in their health, relationships, fertility, family background, finances, career etc. Difficult times take the edges off us.

<u>Questioning Everything</u>

I reassessed my life after we divorced. I hadn't gone to uni because, at the time, money seemed more important. It was something I'd spent many hours wondering about in my early twenties, especially after visits to school friends in their halls, but after getting married I put it to the back of my mind. That time had passed. It's only now, in my late thirties, that I've had time to think about why I wanted to go to uni, what it would have meant to me, and I think really it wasn't so much having the whole university experience, it was that I wanted to teach and I thought a degree was the only pathway to that. But I was wrong. So that's what I'm doing now, I've worked in schools one way or another for over a decade and now I'm learning on the job to be a primary teacher. I am so happy (and tired!), I feel that this is my time now. Sasha, 36.

During the post-divorce reflection period, it's common to question more than just your decision to marry your ex. Everything's thrown into the ring. Any life decision is given a post-mortem, even those that have not been fundamental to your life. I think this is a natural element of the readjustment process, a part of working out what you feel about your marriage is having to decide what you think about everything else. It's framing. Don't be surprised if your choice to study French rather than Spanish at secondary school becomes a source of regret, as well as not having said yes to the boyfriend who suggested inter-railing around Europe for a whole summer and delaying learning to drive until your late twenties. This wondering is a version of playing sliding doors, wondering how your life would have turned out if only you'd taken that flight, gone for dinner with that friend, adopted that dog, stayed on at school, bought that motorbike, just made that different decision.

How do you stop this becoming a regretful pity party? One way to do this is to write it down. Find a notebook and every time one of these 'what if' thoughts arrives, write a story about it. See where your imagination takes you. What does the end of each story tell you about your current desires?

Another method is to find the intent in the wondering. If you find yourself thinking about how you really do wish you'd chosen science A-levels instead of humanities, let's take that further, how do you feel this has held you back? What did you want to do with those different A-levels? Perhaps it's that you always wanted to be a physiotherapist. Okay, and why is that? Maybe it's that you like working with people, you enjoy the sense of achievement in seeing people progress and change, you like a sense of autonomy in your work, you strive for regular hours and a clear idea of what you'll earn as you make headway in your career. It might just be as pure and simple as you really want to be a physiotherapist and have thought about it every day since. Once you find the reasoning for the 'if only' thoughts, you can decide if you want to revisit the end desire, so, in this case, looking into how you might re-train, or how you find a career that satisfies your innate needs. The choice in the past upon which you focus your feelings of regret is rarely the actual change you want to see now.

Saying it Out Loud

I really struggled with the idea that I was a divorcee. It sounded like an old-fashioned word, like 'spinster'. I had to say it out loud to myself when I was alone. I do wonder what anyone would have thought if they could hear me. A grown woman in her forties vacuuming whilst saying 'I am divorced' on repeat. Jill, 47.

Sometimes I wake up in the morning and for that second as I rouse, I forget I'm divorced, and then I remember with a clunk and it shocks me a little bit. It takes my breath away. I never thought this would happen to me. And

I initiated it! I don't write this smugly (there are no winners in divorce), but I can only imagine how it feels to have it sprung upon you. The badge of divorce is a curious one, it seems backwards looking, to be defined by something that occurred years ago. I am at the point now where being divorced is a facet of my story that I am not shy about (speaking to hundreds of women for the purpose of this book being a clear marker!), but it isn't my whole identity. And it doesn't have to be yours either.

If you find it's starting to define you, that you're wearing your marital status, and you don't like the feeling, try not telling new people about it. Remove it from your topic of conversation for a week. See how that feels and find what suits you best.

<u>What Other People Think of You is None of Your Business</u>

I have struggled with accepting that some people see me as the 'baddie' in the divorce. I did have an affair which I am not proud of. But I didn't have an affair lightly. I sound like I am making excuses, which I suppose I am. I have stopped trying to make his family and the school gate gossips forgive me though. I know why I did it. It wasn't just a shag! I did it because I was lonely and because he refused to work as a team. I spent years trying to make it better before I strayed. I wish I had finished the marriage first now as I feel my new relationship is forever tainted, but it is what it is. I had so many years of being lonely and sad that I haven't the time to worry about what other people think of me. Plus, it's a useful device for sorting the wheat from the chaff; the friends who accept what I did are my real friends, they know me and trust my choices. Shauna, 52.

There's a difference between caring what others think of you and obsessing about what others think of you and feeling compelled to seek to change it. You'd have to be an unusual character to not care at all what others' perception of you is; it's human nature, isn't it, to crave the acceptance of other people? But worrying about what those outside your inner circle think of you is not worth your energy. It's no-one else's business what you think of them, and that works both ways.

I feel this is one of the hardest concepts to accept (especially in this time of sharing so much on social media and inviting others' interpretation of our lives), but also one of the most freeing. If you really can come to terms with other people's opinions not being your concern, you can set yourself free of people-pleasing. You know your truth, and if you let go of making others hear it and agree with it, you've ultimately 'won' because you've made a space in your mind for something more worthy. That level of acceptance brings peace and after divorce, that has to be one of our aims, doesn't it?

Give yourself permission to stop trying to change other people's perception of you so that you can focus on being your authentic self. That goes for your ex, family, friends, random mums at the school gates, neighbours, your colleagues etc. Some people will not agree with your divorce, they might blame you and won't forgive you for it. The joke's on them, as you don't need their forgiveness to move on, and remember those who judge others harshly are often giving themselves the exact same punitive treatment. What a way to live! The only person *you* need acceptance from is *you.*

<u>But Others Put Up with Worse</u>

I've pretty much fallen out with my mum over the divorce. She seems to be in competition with me, she keeps saying that being married is hard work and that I should have tried harder, that often marriage isn't about being happy, it's about sticking power. You get the idea. I am not going to repeat the patterns of her marriage and she's angry with me about that. Imogen, 27.

Misery loves company, doesn't it? Some people will see your divorce, specifically your refusal to continue in a relationship that isn't making you happy, as a slur on them and their relationship. After all, they put up with being unhappy, so why shouldn't you? You're going to need to be firm with these friends and family and, rather than justify your decision, shut the conversation down with clear boundary setting. There are lots of ways of doing this, some more bare-faced than others:

1. Turn it back onto them

People like to talk about themselves, so let them. For example, 'yes I'm feeling sad about how my marriage didn't last, tell me what you think is the secret to a long and happy marriage' or 'what would you do if you found out your husband/wife was having an affair?'

2. Make the dodge part of the response

This is a method that takes advantage of social norms and embarrassment;

you basically state that you want to avoid talking about your divorce. For example, 'I find talking about the divorce really upsetting at the moment, shall we talk about something cheerier?'

3. Change the subject

Conversations aren't linear. You only have to listen in to a group of parents looking after toddlers and trying to chat at the same time to witness multiple conversations stopping, starting, branching off, not being finished properly etc. Take advantage of this, for example, 'ah, thanks for asking about the divorce, do you know I've just remembered I had something I wanted to tell you, so you remember how I booked that restaurant for dad's birthday, well…'

4. Leave

If all else fails and they aren't getting the social cues that you don't want to talk about your divorce/ex, make your excuses and leave the room. You might need to go to the loo, you might go and check on the kids, or maybe you will leave the location altogether. Say you forgot about something. This is okay. You don't owe anyone a big discussion about your life.

No Feeling Lasts Forever

At the beginning I was a snotty, puffy mess most of the time. I dream-walked though those months. I didn't think I would recover from the broken feeling. I hadn't seen it coming, which might have been a big part of it. I was properly heartbroken. And then I wasn't. One day I felt like the sun had been turned back on. Lexi, 25.

I am genuinely glad I have experienced divorce. That might sound odd. I am not made of strong stuff; divorce almost broke me. It took me to a place I hadn't been before, but from that place I am more authentically me than I was previously. I am kinder. I am more real. I need less validation from others.

It felt at times like the hellishness of it would last forever. Stuck in a quagmire of internal misery. Rarely, occasionally, I was sure it would take me out, but out of the embers of what felt like hell, I am newly forged. I wouldn't change it, though I would not have believed that I'd feel this way five years ago.

In short, if you are sitting with eyes so engorged it feels they may solder shut and you suspect you have ruined your life, please know you won't always feel like that. The one thing that you can rely upon is that no feeling lasts forever.

Coping with the Nights

In the early months I kept myself busy in the day and it was fine. I was able to hold it together for my daughters, I was the model employee – so attentive. After the girls went to bed and I'd done the lunchboxes for the next day, put a wash on, done the ironing, tidied up, I'd sit down and the hours between then and the morning felt so long. I'd try to focus on the TV, but nothing stopped my mind from wandering. I was a menace texting friends and family. I was very lonely and it was a hard time. I wish I had a magic wand for other women, but I just think you have to go through it. One night as I was brushing my teeth, I realised that the evening hadn't been an ordeal and then when that happened more than it didn't, I knew the healing was underway. Anita, 36.

If you have children, the evenings are the loneliest time when you're a newly single parent. They're tucked up in bed, the day is over, and you're left with your thoughts. I found the evening and nights (gah, the insomnia!) the hardest part of my post-divorce life. Tears were most definitely shed. My bed was too large. I placed a pillow next to me, a feathery version of a husband to make the space less expansive. The nights stretched out, bending time into a bigger space than felt possible. Of an evening I was too tired and wrung-out to do very much, but also not doing much left my brain to push through to catastrophe mode. I scrolled social media a lot, read numerous online newspaper articles, I used the TV as company though I often found concentrating in anything longer than 15-minute blocks impossible. Like Anita says, I just had to go through it.

Learning a new skill can be a good distraction; many women I have spoken to said that keeping their hands and mind busy learning to crochet/knit was a lifesaver. Others preferred jigsaws, watching the whole back catalogue of *Silent Witness*, learning to perfect French patisserie, hammering YouTube yoga classes and even scribbling in adult colouring books. The thing to remember is that it's okay to use a new hobby to pass the time and NOT continue with it. You don't have to commit to anything long term, just find what works for you.

The Severance Act

He took the girls to Rainbows on Thursday night and dropped them back like he always did, put them to bed and said goodnight. I said goodbye, it was all the same as usual. The next morning, I was just getting the girls into the car with all their school paraphernalia and I realised he hadn't put the bins out the night before, like he always did. The bin men come super early on our street so that meant we'd missed the pick-up. I was so angry with him and then, after typing a furious text, I thought better of it and didn't send it. Actually, he didn't live here anymore. He was soon to be my ex-husband and I needed to put my own bins out. It was such a crunch moment. A real 'this is it' realisation. Ella, 32.

There's a point in every woman's divorce process where she realises that the relationship she previously had with her ex has gone forever. For me it was a teaspoon that did it. We were out having lunch with our sons and ordered one pudding to share as it was quite rich and everyone said they were pretty full. I ate a small sliver of the chocolate mousse with the one teaspoon provided and then offered it to him. He used his coffee spoon instead. I don't know why it hadn't occurred to me that he may not want to share saliva with me anymore given we were pretty far into the divorce process and he had a new partner. It just hadn't. It was a real turning point in the separation though, a severance act if you will.

In short, don't expect a man who has been given notice of his spousal services no longer being required, to act like a husband. He won't. Or if he does, be suspicious.

Big Girl Pants

I've always felt immature, despite presenting well. When I realised my marriage was beyond salvation it was a shock to the system, not least because I knew the only person who could deal with the fall-out was me. I think it took getting divorced for me to finally grow up and be an adult. Jessie, 33.

I think everyone who gets divorced at some point dreams that a fairy godmother will arrive and sort the whole sorry mess out. I remember saying to a friend, through tears, 'I just want someone to look after me, take all this away and deal with it.' The friend in question just nodded. Of course friends and family can support you in a myriad of ways, but, really, you have to put on your big girl pants and crack on. It's the same realisation I had when in labour each time; that you can have the best birth partner, a wonderful midwife, amazing pain relief, but really, when it comes down to it, you're on your own. Ultimately you do divorce alone too, in that the emotional journey you're on is yours and your alone. A solitary one. There is such strength in doing things alone though.

<u>STIs</u>

I went to get tested because my sister was badgering me about it. She had a friend who had contracted herpes after a one-night stand and was obsessed with the fact my ex might have passed something like that onto me. I really only went to stop her nagging. No one was more surprised than me when my results came back and I had chlamydia. I let my ex know, or rather I screamed down the phone at my ex that he had infected me. He denied it and actually accused me of cheating. All's well that ends well, I got prescribed some drugs to get rid of it. Good job my sister is so persistent really. Elise, 28.

If you suspect even for one tiny second that you have been cheated on, get a test. It's not like it was when we were teenagers, I promise you. They don't swab your urethra anymore and ask you for a full breakdown of every person you've ever held hands with. Instead, they take a small amount of history, some blood and give you a swab to use on your own vagina, in a private room. The results come by text, post or phone call, you decide. (The details vary by county, but basically this is how it works nowadays.)

I know it's scary. I know it seems like a waste of time, especially when a lot of the NHS services only run an appointment system on certain days, at restricted times. I know you're busy and that waiting in a room with under-15s feels sordid and unjust. Top tips: don't put it off (getting the results feels like a clean slate) and take a friend with you if you can. It's not your fault if you have been put at risk. It is your fault if you wilfully ignore the risk.

<u>Rose-Tinted Glasses</u>

I had a tendency after he left to only remember the good times. All the fun nights out before we had kids, the holidays abroad, the laughs, the amazing sex, the way he used to look at me that made my stomach flip. All the lovely memories that I feel sad won't be repeated. A few months after we separated, he lied to me about why he couldn't have the kids overnight, and it triggered how I used to feel when I knew he was being dishonest, which was frequent towards the end. Then I started to join the dots that pretty much all our good times involved him being quite drunk. I don't see it as a glorious relationship now, I see it as an average marriage with more downs than ups. Naomi, 33.

It's wise to approach your marital memories with balance. It's as bad for you to only see the negative points of your marriage as it is to only see the positive. One thing's for sure, romanticising your relationship is bad for your mental health. Stop doing it. It ended for a reason. If you can't remember why in the wee small hours of the morning, utilise The Nob List, page 201.

Places of Solace

I was brought up as a Catholic but haven't practised for many years. I felt drawn back to the church during the end of my marriage. Not in a religious way, but I think because it felt familiar and comforting to me. Mimi, 32.

I'm not a religious person, though I do quite enjoy the community of the church and love to belt out a hymn or two. In the first few months after I separated, the local church became a place of solace for me. It was the only space I could find to hold my grief. I didn't want anyone or anything to take my hurt away. I couldn't be made better or consoled, and so the church sat with me in my grief whilst I sat literally within it. The quietness and calm stilled me. I felt wrapped up by the pew. As I left after each service, the priest touched my shoulder and every time it made me cry. Just that simple act of kindness made me feel understood, and yet I hadn't chatted to anyone. Sitting with my grief felt better than speaking it.

I have spoken to many women who found quiet spaces became special to them – a tonic during the period when they were grieving their marriage. For one the local reservoir. For another the ruins of a castle. One woman liked to sit in the local graveyard. Another enjoyed visiting her local zoo and sitting in the reptile house. Many sat in their gardens late at night, alone. Whatever gets you through.

The Importance of Touch

I have missed the touch of another person so much. It sounds like a small thing, but when you no longer have young children at home and when your husband leaves, it can be hard to literally reach out to other people. I have never been much of a hugger of friends, so have had to make an effort to be more touchy-feely. I have even started to have regular reflexology sessions which I tell people is about self-care, but I think it's the touch element that I need. Ina, 59.

If you find yourself living alone after getting divorced, don't underestimate how the absence of touch can affect you. Being touched by another human soothes us (literally – it calms our heart rate, activates the vagus nerve linked to how compassionate we feel and can release oxytocin, the love hormone), and makes us feel safe. Touch doesn't have to be between romantic partners, it can be a hug with a friend, a shampoo and scalp massage with your hairdresser, dancing with a partner at a class, having a massage, stroking a cat/dog. Connection is good for us.

Maintaining the Peace

I am very careful how I email and text him. I know he has struggled to cope with me having a new partner and I don't want to rub his nose in it. I am kind and, if I am honest, try to make him feel like the big man still. He is wounded and not over it all yet. Being calm has kept relations between us civil, which is best for the children at the end of the day. Candice, 47.

How you communicate is everything. If you know your ex rubs you up the wrong way, make a pact with yourself to only reply to them after sleeping on your drafted response. You will save yourself potentially hours of arguing, upset and even money (in legal fees) if you can sit on your hands and press send another day. Bonus points if you can turn how you see this upside down, from needing to placate them by spacing out and dampening down your communications, to having the opportunity to not have immediate contact with someone who pisses you off.

If you have been the initiator of the divorce, remember that your ex may be hurting long, long after you are feeling fine. They are still gathering themselves and in pain. Being kind isn't just for them, it's for you, it's for your kids and it's so that when the dust settles you can look back without blushing regrets.

Think of them as the child they once were, facing rejection. Before you send an email or text, read it out as if your worst enemy were reading it. In a snarky, bitchy, whiny voice. That's the worst case scenario of how your ex reads your emails. Edit accordingly.

Wedding Paraphernalia

I hung onto my wedding dress for four years before I decided it was just taking up a lot of room in my wardrobe and needed to go. Maybe it helped that I have sons and not daughters, so it never occurred to me that they might want to wear it to their own wedding one day (actually I guess they might… who knows). Anyway, regardless of whether the boys wanted to wear my dress, I didn't want them to. It had too many negative connotations. I sold it through a wedding boutique who had a service to sell on pre-loved dresses. I managed to get £600 for it, so with their fee about £500. I spent it on a spa weekend with my best friend. It was glorious and I now have more room for my new single wardrobe. Lorna, 36.

What you do with the various wedding detritus will be influenced by whether there are children from the marriage. The love story of how they came to be *is* important, even if it isn't to them right now. It might be tempting to burn the wedding albums, but your relationship is part of your children's lives, so whilst I personally feel keeping photos of your big day on the walls is a bit odd, I think you need to hold onto some of the photos for your kids, albeit perhaps not on display. I put all the photos, cards, menus, wedding ring and the like into a box and taped it up. It's in a safe place for my sons if they want to look at it when they're older. The dress was less of an issue as it was a black and white spotty number that cost £55 from an unnamed shop on Brick Lane. It's living a new life with someone who bought it from the local Mind charity shop now. I hope they'll be very happy together; it was a great dress and our wedding was a wonderful day. In fact, on my wedding anniversary I now try to do something giving. One year I gave blood, another year donated to the food bank, next year, not sure yet, but I'll do something to mark it.

There are lots of options of what to do with wedding jewellery and clothing. Many women have their wedding band melted down and made into a new piece of jewellery, lots symbolically throw them into the sea/river, some sell their rings for some much-needed cash. Dresses are burnt, binned, wrecked (in a 'trash the dress' type ceremony), dyed a new colour to live again as ballgowns, given to Gift of a Wedding charity who organise weddings for the terminally ill, and even donated to local amateur dramatic societies to be worn in multiple future make-believe ceremonies. Your way is the right way, just be respectful to your children if you have them. Watching their mum pour petrol over their wedding dress isn't what happy childhood memories are made of.

<u>Chattels</u>

In the divorce process, we tried to split all the furniture and kitchen stuff and, well, everything, but it didn't go smoothly. He decided to get his solicitor involved and issued a list of what he wanted. I was on the verge of spending money with my solicitor replying with a myriad of reasons why I wanted some of the items and then I had a moment of clarity. I realised I didn't actually want anything that was a product of our marriage. We hadn't been married for very long, a lot of what we owned together had been wedding presents and I didn't want to use our nice Le Creuset pan and think to how his aunt had bought that from our gift list. I emailed him and said I thought he should take everything from the list and left it there. Some of my friends thought I was mad, but I needed to start afresh. I don't regret it for a moment. Cherry, 27.

The memories inanimate objects hold, eh? There's a set of saucepans I still use that belonged to my ex-husband. Every time I put one on the stove, I think of him. (I should add he elected not to take these with him; I am not holding the pans hostage.) They need to go, really. There's nothing wrong with them, in fact they're an excellent set of pans, but my do they spark memories.

For me objects and places hold a lot of meaning. Some restaurants I won't eat in again because the memories are too strong. Perhaps that will fade in the future. If it doesn't, that's okay. I went through a process of slowly replacing most furniture in my home after the split, it was important to me. The only things I really wanted were the items I had brought into the marriage with me at the start, and of course anything related to the children. For others, the chattels of marriage have little meaning. They're just things.

If you find yourself fighting over objects from the marriage, take a moment to consider if this is about the item or about winning. Making a list of the things you definitely need, the 'nice to keep' pile, the 'very expensive and should we sell?' lot and the 'don't cares' is helpful and gives you a focus when negotiating.

New Things to Buy

He had chosen the cutlery and it had always been so heavy to hold, especially for the kids. I became obsessed with finding the perfect cutlery set to replace it. Every shop I went to, I'd always see if they had nice knives and forks. In the end, I found the perfect set in Ikea of all places. I bought enough for having friends over for dinner and can tell you it was a moment of joy to pop all the heavy cutlery he chose into a box and take it to my local charity shop. A literal and metaphorical weight had been lifted. Rose, 40.

You may be overcome with an overwhelming urge to replace everything in your home. You may even be obsessed with replacing your home (or you may have to as part of splitting assets) due to the memories, happy and sad. Who knew that the happy memories would be the hardest of all?

I felt the need to purge in many ways and got rid of or replaced a lot. I can tell you, with the benefit of many an expensive mistake, that the things that have brought me joy and peace have been:

- A set of new door locks (though remember if you have older children that them taking the new keys to your ex's house could mean they get copied)
- A new bed frame and mattress
- A new sofa suitable for proper lounging on
- A lick of paint in colours that crucially only I like. Bright-green kitchen? Hell, yeah!
- A toolkit

There is something really quite calming about sleeping in a bed that you and your ex have not slept in or had sex in together. So if funds are limited, this would be my priority.

Social Media

I felt like I'd lost about ten years in age when I left him. Light and happy and reborn, I guess. All the clichés. I started dating much younger men, had a few one-night stands; I had such a good time. I wouldn't change any of it, except I so wish I hadn't plastered it all over Facebook and Instagram. After one especially nasty solicitor's letter, I even posted a long rant on Facebook about how awful he was being. People I thought were my friends showed him and it added fuel to the fire. I think the whole thing would have been much less painful for everyone if I'd just kept my nights out and feelings to myself. Leila, 33.

We all share elements of our lives. And with any separation and the inevitable rebirth and sense of freedom it gives, you may find yourself wanting to share these feelings online. You're free! You can do what you bloody well want! You can tell the world about your new boyfriend! You can tell the world about your crap marriage and how it was all a sham! Except, just no.

Don't do it.

But…?

No. Don't do it.

But…what about?

Seriously, don't do it. Best-case scenario is your ex doesn't see it, the friends you retained in the split do, and they think you're an idiot.

Worst-case scenario is that you think your ex hasn't seen it, but he is actually following you under a pseudonym (or a 'friend' shows him your posts) and it is used against you at a later date in court or otherwise.

Just don't do it. It's not worth it. Think about how it would feel the other way round and do as you would be done by. Also it's very drama-llama-esque and we always aim higher than that. There is dignity in silence. Yes, you want everyone to know what a nob he is, but really silence is just so bloody damning.

<u>He's a Fake and a Phony and I Wish I'd Never Laid Eyes on Him</u>

After 22 years of marriage, I thought I knew my husband really well. He and I had grown up together and sort of merged. I often knew what he was about to say before he did. His mannerisms and sayings were familiar. He felt comfortable. When he sat me down and said he was leaving I was utterly shocked. I never thought this would happen to me. It's been very hard to cope with the change but far and away the worst thing has been seeing him morph into a completely different person. He met his new wife very quickly after we split (I am pretty sure she was the reason for him leaving but he assures me not) and started dressing much younger, speaking with a slightly different intonation, using new sayings and changing his outlook on almost everything. Suddenly he was obsessed with the paleo diet. I feel like he was just pretending to be who he was when we were married. It feels like it was all a sham. Niamh, 51.

Ah, the immortal words of Sandy from *Grease!* There's something quite disturbing about watching the person you thought you knew inside out, knew so well you could predict their next words, turn into someone you know isn't them. It feels so fake and disingenuous.

Some people don't have a very strong sense of self and so they kind of borrow from their partners and friends along their journey through life. Picking up their sayings, their mannerisms, their dress sense, their approach to being. It's just a part of who they are; in fact, this cherry picking *is* one of their traits. And so, if you watch the man who used to be your sidekick become a different version of himself after meeting a new partner, grit your teeth and try not to rise to the changes.

Because he is not necessarily fake, just not the version of him *you* knew. This version is not yours; he is hers. So you don't recognise him. And that hurts. But she would not recognise the man you once knew either. We are all different to different people.

It is very tempting to point out that your ex clearly has no personality of his own. That he is fake. Don't do it. It's unpleasant and unnecessary. Always take the higher moral ground, not because he deserves it necessarily, but because it feels good to you.

<u>When he Remarries</u>

If you had told me in the early days I would feel no emotion, positive or negative, when my ex told me he was getting married again, I would not have believed you. But that's exactly what happened. His second wife is lovely, we get along well and manage to co-parent the children calmly and with genuine understanding. I hope they are happy together, but I don't feel jealous of her. He and I didn't work well, whereas he and his wife do. I actually see our marriage as his starter marriage. As for me, I don't think I will marry again, but never say never. Flic, 37.

You'll notice I named this 'when he remarries' and not 'if he remarries', mainly because men are twice as likely as women to marry again after divorcing (ONS Marriages in England and Wales, 2013). That doesn't mean divorced women aren't going on to have relationships, just that they may not cohabit with their new partner or may live together without marrying.

Whatever your feelings are about your ex remarrying, whether you get along with him and his wife-to-be and wish them a life of happiness together or whether you hope she gets the shits as she walks down the aisle, try not to see the new wife as the victor. Sure, if he had an affair, being the second wife might feel triumphant to her ('he chose me!'), but it might also feel like being second best; after all, he chose someone else first.

Ultimately, his marriage with his second/third/fourth wife is their love story, it isn't part of your love story. And people really don't change. If he was a pain with you, you can bet he will be with her. The honeymoon period is named after a short break from reality for a reason.

Oh and if he constantly uses 'we' in all his communications with you once he has a new partner/spouse, try not to let it irritate you. It's the sign of a weak sense of self. He's struggling with taking responsibility for his own actions and decisions. Not your problem. In fact, hers now.

Everything You Aren't

He was always really unpleasant about short women, used to call them PORGS (people of restricted growth) which he thought was funny, and was also quite bitchy about anyone overweight. Used to make comments under his breath about larger women if we walked past them. Imagine my surprise when he sent his new very short and quite plump girlfriend to collect the kids one Friday. I am really perplexed by it as he couldn't even get an erection when I was a bit bigger after having the girls. Maybe it was me. Lily, 39.

I have a slightly different take on this to a lot of people. I think if an ex-partner of mine were to get into a relationship with someone who was very similar in looks and personality to me I'd be disturbed. It would signify to me that the connection we had together wasn't a unique alchemy that existed, more that I was just physically his type. If your ex gets into a relationship with someone who is very different to you, take it to mean that it was the essence of you that they were attracted to when you first met, just as it's the essence of their new partner they are attracted to now.

When I was at university, I once met in the loos of a club the ex-girlfriend of my then boyfriend. We had an extremely similar look, so much so that we both stood and took stock of each other. Now that was a bit of a galling moment. His interest in me (and her) felt skin deep.

Your Clitoris May Betray You

The worst thing about my ex is that he's really attractive. And, annoyingly, I still have a full body response to him. He comes to pick the kids up and, as I hear his car in the drive, I can feel myself tingle all over. I hate myself for it, but it's completely involuntary. When he texts me, again, about the kids, I actually get a bit, well, not sure how to say this, but, excited. I really wish it didn't happen. It makes me feel like maybe I made the wrong decision. I know I didn't deep down as he was a nightmare, but my body thinks otherwise. Jody, 38.

I have heard so many women admit to still (involuntarily) finding their ex attractive, their body completely betraying their rational mind. Listen, you really must not beat yourself up over this. We have all found inappropriate people attractive. My list, over the years, has included Michael Portillo, Richard Madeley and a priest who was especially kind to me. It doesn't mean I would want to be in a relationship with any of them, it doesn't even mean I want to have sex with them, it's just a physical reaction.

Dreams of Murder

It started off as a violent dream where I set his feet in a block of cement and then left him to rot. I woke up sweating and feeling guilty, but also quite thrilled at the thought of him being dead. He was very difficult in the divorce and I'll admit at times I fantasised about him dying in a car crash. He always drove like a fool and had to travel a lot for work, so when I saw news of a crash on the motorway, I'd hope it was him. I'm really not a horrible person, and I feel awful that I had these thoughts. He was just such a nightmare, I wanted him to disappear. Frances, 52.

I am going to tell you a secret. It is completely normal to fantasize about the death of your ex. In fact, to take it a step further, it is completely normal to fantasize about killing your ex. I have lost count of the number of times women have whispered this confession to me. Some even started to look into the cost of a hitman. Crucially, none of them did it. So please don't feel guilty for thinking these things. I'd suggest it's better to acknowledge why you feel them, than bury them with guilt and self-hatred at what an awful person you must be. The desire for an ex to disappear is just a symptom of how incredibly hard you are finding the break-up; a wish for things to be neater and cleaner. Death would be easier to mourn than a divorce for some. It doesn't make you the star of *Luther*'s next storyline.

<u>Death of the Ex-Spouse</u>

He's been a very tricky man to divorce. Some of the things he's said to our daughter about me are wicked. Lies upon lies. The thing that irritates me the most is, given he is 25 years older than me (yes that's the last time I ever marry someone old enough to be my father), and also in pretty bad health, there's a strong possibility I will have to counsel our daughter over his death. And I hate him! But I will have to be kind and sympathetic and understanding. I could scream! Natasha, 40.

If you have children with your ex, there's a realisation at some point that your relationship with them never ends. Not even if they die! They're a part of your child forevermore and if your child doesn't have siblings, they will need your input into how they remember the relationship with your ex (after they die or if they leave and are ostensibly absent) even more than if they had brothers and sisters. It's another moment of remembering that you can be friendly with your offspring, but they are not your best friend and confidante and, no matter what their father did or didn't do, it's likely they love them on some level; you need to find a way to honour that with them.

<u>Choose to Forgive Everyday</u>

It took an Instagram meme to make me realise I was spending all my energy on hating him for splitting our family up and that I had to forgive him for my own wellbeing. I was eaten up with anger and it wasn't serving anyone. He didn't care! I doubt he even noticed. I am in a better space now I have let go. Erika, 45.

Forgiving is hard, isn't it? Holding onto resentment involves an element of winning. ('See how hurt I am, see what damage they did to me, see how bad they are!') By letting go, you haven't relinquished this. You are still allowed to have been hurt, those feelings still happened and still matter.

If you're finding it hard to forgive (and that includes forgiving yourself too), consider the alternative. You hold onto the hate and the anger and you're stuck at that point in time. Everyone else will move on except for you, still hurting, still unable to forgive. You're the one who's being punished. It's not a case of having to forgive *and* forget, you can forgive and never trust that person again, but by holding onto the hatred and refusing to let go, you're alone in a kind of purgatory. You don't deserve that.

Channelling your Inner Pollyanna

I have stopped being a Sad Sack and started to look at life in a glass half full way. Yes, I don't have another adult living in the house to split the chores with, but instead I don't have to moan at another adult to do their share of the chores. Likewise, I don't have anyone to share the parental load with, but I get to say yes to my daughter's request at playdates and park trips after school, things he didn't like or encourage. Life is simpler in many ways and I thank myself for that regularly. Jemima, 29.

If you can move your mindset from obligation to opportunity, you will have a more content life. So every time you think 'I have to', try and change it to 'I get to'. It's such a tiny shift, but it's a gamechanger.

For me in the early days of separation I found it very hard to adjust to my sons not being at home at weekends. I missed the noise and the chaos. To move forwards and look after my own mental health, I had to stop seeing those weekends for all the moments I'd lost and instead see the opportunity. One weekend I managed to paint the stairs, something that would have been nigh on impossible with three sets of small feet trampling past every few minutes. I also caught up on years of sleep deprivation, something my married friends didn't have the chance to do. I needed that rest so much. One small change in my language helped to remind me that there *is* joy to be found in most situations. Try writing down your 'I get to' moments on page 203 and see how they snowball once you make the shift.

Mirror, Mirror

I look back at my first marriage now and laugh. Thank goodness we didn't have children. I didn't even know who I was. I was 23 when we got married, way too young in hindsight. I was ashamed of my background which is quite poor. I was working as an admin assistant for an investment bank, researching for meetings, photocopying and binding, the usual boring stuff. I watched all the other posh but dim admin assistants get asked out by the rich bankers and thought I wanted a bit of that. So I imitated them. And it only bloody worked! I had a whirlwind romance with a man called Piers. We got married 6 months after our first date and my God was he awful. Really not nice and very fake to be honest. His real name wasn't even Piers, he'd changed it. His real name was Ross. We lasted 8 months until I realised I couldn't cope with how exhausting it was being something I wasn't. I had pretended to be a posh slightly thick girl, but I'm not. I'm quite clever really, canny I'd say, and working class through and through. We split, I left the bank and started up a food stall. We've just had one of our products listed in Waitrose and my boyfriend works for the design agency I commissioned to develop the new branding. I am my true self and the memories of Piers (sorry, Ross) and his banker mates are distant now. I will definitely marry again, I am sure, but it'll be for the right reasons next time. Evie, 26.

One of my main complaints about previous relationships is that I have had more than one long-term partnership with men who have an interesting relationship with the truth. From the seemingly meaningless ('my train was cancelled so we stayed in the pub') to the downright shocking ('I have terminal throat cancer') Yes, really! Not sure how the culprit was planning on his impending death not occurring given the survival rates for the stage 4 cancer he'd chosen for himself.

I saw myself as someone who attracted men who lie. But hang on, it is only in later life I have been able to face a very difficult truth. That what we attract is often what we put out. I'm not confessing to lying about having a terminal illness. I'm telling you that the little lies I told myself and the world attracted the bigger liars.

In my twenties, I lived in London and worked in advertising. When I look back at it now, I was actually deeply unhappy, lonely and lost. I felt rudderless. Years after moving to the capital, I watched on as other people established close social groups and a sense of community. I didn't have this and I just didn't understand how it had passed me by. I was so deeply lonely, I sometimes sat on the end of my bed on a Saturday night and howled. And no one heard, no one cared. Maybe the people upstairs did, actually, they might have found the commotion annoying. So what did I do? Find my tribe? Join clubs? Try night classes? Nope.

I internet dated with such gusto it was exhausting. The loneliness deepened as these one- night-only dates felt lacking in any connection or kindness. One man even stole my purse from me and instead of confronting him, I was so ashamed and embarrassed that I excused myself, called my flatmate and asked that he meet me at our door to pay for my taxi. Another man, a casual 'boyfriend', raped me. And did I report it? I did not. I was too ashamed. I even saw him again socially.

Another man, my boss in fact, played with my emotions for years. He knew I had feelings for him and yet took me out for drinks, chatted to me, emailed me, flirted. But never even a kiss. I put up with this because, hey, I was a cool kind of girl, I was okay with him and I hanging out just as pals. I was okay with him using me to bolster his ego. It didn't matter that these small scraps of affection made me feel like a second-class citizen. It was okay that he even instructed my bridesmaid to tell me on my wedding day 'it should have been me'. It wasn't okay. It hurt.

Why am I telling you this? Because I didn't tell anyone else. I was so ashamed. I was so embarrassed. What did I do? I lied to everyone and said my life was great. And that was how I became so vulnerable, because I was getting back what I was putting out. My lack of authenticity was reflected back in the men who liked me. So my hard-earned wisdom is to be your true self, whatever you do. Be your authentic self, however painful it is at times.

<u>Regressing</u>

I know a lot of people say that divorce ages you but I think it's done the opposite to me. I have a few more worry lines from it, but my behaviour has been positively childish since the split. I've been surviving on Pot Noodles, Malibu and Diet Coke, smoking on nights out, texting inappropriate men and buying lots of new going-out dresses, despite not actually going out enough to wear them all. Freya, 43.

Lots of women report that after their marriage ended, they found themselves behaving in much the same way as when they were last single. Which isn't such a change in behaviour if you were married for two years after a whirlwind courtship, but if the last time you were single was 1982 and you were 16 then, it can be surprising for your nearest and dearest to witness. Like a teenage version of you re-emerging in a mid-fifties body. Women have told me their grown-up children have been irritated by this transformation, with the tables turning so that they hide in the garden smoking fags when their offspring are in bed, and stay out until 2am dancing the night away much to their children's disgust. Many have experienced the safe sex chat from their adult sons and daughters, despite having delivered this very same lecture to them less than a decade previously.

This regression of behaviour can also extend into those initial romantic dealings after your marriage ends. In my first post-divorce weekend away with my boyfriend, I found myself pushing to play out long-forgotten teenage relationship dynamics. The result was a massive jealousy-induced row in a loft room in Poland about someone he had slept with 15 years previously, where the madness of it ended in an agreement to split up. It was over the top, silly and done with a half-arsed lack of intention, pretty much playing out some of the behaviour of the last time I was single. We are creatures of habit and it's highly likely when you enter into another relationship, the same patterns will play out, maybe even some from your marriage. Being aware of the patterns and working out how they serve you is the key. Are they useful? Or keeping you stuck?

Me, I had to go all the way to Eastern Europe to resurrect my long-buried teenage self and to realise that I was too old and too tired for all that nonsense of taking a relationship to the brink of failure in order to believe it was worth fighting for. We made up and vowed not to have another argument like that. And we haven't.

<u>Back in the Game</u>

I know everyone says not to jump into a new relationship straight after getting divorced but for me it was what I needed and was really positive. It was completely on my terms and a lot of fun. It didn't work out, but I'm fine with that. It taught me that I am loveable and sexy and that I deserve to be happy. I was the one who finished it, but we've remained in touch. It's so damned healthy compared to my marriage break-up. Bina, 27.

I know it's something of a platitude to say that, once you've reached rock bottom, you have nothing left to lose, but, hey, there's truth in it. When you've had your heart trampled on and found it difficult to catch your breath because you're so broken inside, it can make you fearless in jumping straight back into a relationship. There is no 'one size fits all' when it comes to getting back in the game; you don't have to sit about and lick your wounds for a requisite period of time.

Less than six months after my decree absolute landed on the doormat, I found myself in a relationship with a younger man who had such a reputation, a friend said to me 'I know so many people who've slept with him, but I don't get it myself.' Yes, really. Now, previously I would never have been up for a relationship with a younger man with a promiscuous past. I would have felt too insecure, too exposed by his youth and experience. And yet I jumped in. I remember thinking that I was so low that I didn't care if I got hurt. There was something masochistic yet liberating about this fatalistic approach. The miserable, poetic ending I expected didn't happen. But if it had, I knew I could handle it, I'd done it before more than once.

Wary

I've been guilty of putting up a wall around me since the divorce. I was so hurt by my marriage ending, I find it difficult to trust anyone now. My ex-husband was my childhood sweetheart and I am not sure I will ever love anyone in the same way again, though that might be a good thing given how things turned out. Renee, 50.

For every person who feels that sense of abandonment of being able to jump straight into a new relationship (see above), there's another who will be wary, especially when a divorce has been acrimonious. To have known extreme kindness and tenderness from the same person who then seemed determined to destroy you (whether with or without intent) makes accepting kindness from the next person a gamble. Those first feelings of love and discovery don't feel quite so sweet from your next love. They can feel like the foreword to a long campaign of misery.

If this is how you feel, take things slowly and express yourself. If they're the right fit for you, they'll understand and wait. If they're pushing the relationship forward despite your protestations, have a read of Red Flags, (page 121) and be honest with yourself whether this person is good news. Sometimes we're wary because our intuition is trying to tell us something.

When You're Not Ready Yet

I had this massive need to go out and drink wine with my girlfriends, but I could not entertain speaking to single men. I wasn't ready for a good year. One of my friends used to annoyingly tell any man who approached our group that I was newly single. I think she was hoping to live vicariously through me hooking up with random men. In the end I had to talk to her about it and ask her not to. I started dating when I was ready and not a moment before. Verity, 39.

You decide when you're ready. Not your friends, not your family, not your ex from when you were at secondary school who's heard you're back on the market and thinks he might have another crack. No, no, no. It's on your terms.

I didn't realise until I separated from my ex how much a ring on your wedding finger wards off would-be suitors. A bare finger was some is a form of green light. So I found an old ring given to me by my grandmother for my 21st birthday and wore that on nights out. It's a shame that this kind of overt display of male ownership is necessary, but, for me, I needed to re-group and that wasn't going to happen talking to random men. It was a shorthand way of communicating that I wasn't approachable.

Online Dating

Having last been single before dating apps were a thing, it was such a huge change. I felt like I was doing the online shop, swiping away, perusing what was available. Needless to say, a lot of the men I went on dates with did not live up to the expectation of their profile photo, but it was good fun for a while. After what seemed like hundreds of mediocre dates, I met my current partner through a pottery course I booked myself onto as a post-divorce treat. Polly, 45.

If you decide to dip your toe into the world of online dating, then brace yourself. It's a looking-glass into the whole of society, meaning it's a smorgasbord of characters. Lovely, odd, shy, downright nasty, damaged, rich, beautiful, loud, abusive, kind, ugly, charismatic, poor, monosyllabic, crude, super intelligent, not-so-bright and everything in between. If they exist, they're online and they're looking to meet someone.

You need to protect your heart when you date online. Having done a lot of online dating (pre Tinder/Bumble/Hinge etc., admittedly), here's my advice, for what it's worth:

1. Not everyone online wants to actually meet. Some people use it as a free sexting service or a way to massage their ego. You can invest hours and hours in messaging someone to find they never had any intention of meeting in real life. You can also find after messaging too much that you build an idea of who the person is in your head and it's a bit of a shock when their actual persona isn't like the one you constructed for them.

2. Not everyone is single. Yes, there are a lot of people using dating apps to have affairs. Trust your gut instinct.

3. People lie about their age and often search for potential partners outside of their own age group. So as a 41 year old, I might shave two years off my age and be 39, then search for men who are 45– 55. These men have likely shaved a few years off their age themselves and may be pushing 60. Maybe it all evens out in the end?

4. People upload their best photos, not their most representative, so be prepared to be a bit surprised. When it comes to apps, people spend just seconds deciding whether to swipe left or right, so I guess you can't blame people for using their best photos, even if they were taken over 15 years ago.

5. People lie about things other than their age. Like their height. I know, what an idiotic lie. It's not like you wouldn't notice, is it?

6. Ghosting is the way many people end a relationship now. What is it? Simply cutting off all communication with someone you have been sleeping with/dating/messaging with no reason given. They become like a ghost and just disappear. Don't take it personally. It's a very lucky escape from someone who is not emotionally mature. Take it as a gift, not an insult.

7. Lots of people use dating apps to find no-strings-attached sex, but are not honest about their intentions.

8. You do not have to answer every single message. You will feel compelled to at first because you're probably polite and well-mannered. Listen to me, please: you don't have to reply to everyone. Maybe you don't like the look of the person, you find their message distasteful, where they're located isn't

convenient, any reason is valid. You don't owe a stranger on the internet anything.

9. Hedge your bets and look outside of dating apps too. There are amazing people everywhere.

10. Safety first, always. Never give out your address, place of work, the school(s) your child(ren) attend, your surname etc. If you are going to meet someone in real life who you've met online, you must let someone know where you're going, get them to call you during the date as a get-out opportunity, ensure it's a public place and, please, don't go home with them until you know them well. If your intuition is shouting at you that something isn't right, leave.

Sex; Not With Your Ex

I had this strange experience the first time I had sex with a new partner. It was a strong sensation of having cheated on my ex. I felt so guilty, like I had betrayed him and our marriage. We had been divorced for months by the time I slept with someone new, so it wasn't an emotion based in reality. I blushed when I saw my ex the next time, I felt like he knew what I'd done 'behind his back'. Elise, 46.

This sense of having cheated on your ex-husband once he's no longer the last person you slept with seems to especially afflict women who had children with their ex. Perhaps being physically affectionate to a man other than their children's father feels like betraying the family unit (rather than cheating on the ex)?

And comparing sex with a new partner to the sex with your ex is to be expected. Don't feel guilty. Prepare yourself that it might be a let-down. In a long marriage you learn what your spouse likes, what they don't. You can't expect a new lover to intrinsically know what makes you tick. (Though of course they may well do). The fun is in the discovery. The memories of sex with your ex will fade in time so that, eventually, you can barely remember it.

A New Blueprint for Love

My boyfriend and I have a completely different type of relationship to the one I had with my ex-husband. My ex and I led quite separate lives; we didn't even watch TV in the same room! This time around I'm part of a couple who exercise together for goodness sake! I feel like I have been able to start from scratch and shape a relationship on my terms. I'm a lot happier, mainly because I am not compromising now. I know who I am and have stopped pretending to be someone else to please a man. My boyfriend and I are just a better match in every way. Robyn, 30.

Getting divorced is an opportunity to take the good bits of your relationship with you and leave the bad behind. You get to decide how you are formed from your divorce and, importantly, what you want in your next partner. In fact, you get to decide if there will even be a next partner. Moving on can be deciding not to have another live-in long-term romantic relationship.

Just because your last relationship was one that involved being married, does not mean it has to be the Big Love Story of your life. It really doesn't, even if it's the source of where your beautiful children came from. Your marriage might have spanned 40 years, but you can still have another love story, a much shorter one, that fulfils you more fully than anything that came before it. Length of time does not make for a more worthy experience.

It's all so personal. For me, I am less sure of longevity since I divorced; I don't look at my current relationship and assume anything. I also don't feel scared that it may not last until the day I die. I accept the love I receive from it as a bonus. That doesn't mean I am not sure of it, I just don't try to put constraints on it. I hope it lasts, but, if it doesn't, I will be okay. He does not make me whole. I am already a whole person. This approach is mine, it's not right or wrong, just the way I am doing things now. I know that if I had read this paragraph when married I would have thought it was sad. I don't now, I find it powerful.

What I do know is that I love being loved. I want to be loved all the time; I want all the love! It's insatiable and thirsty and feels optimistic. Every bit of me is loved, even the annoying and difficult stuff. Through this relationship and possibly through aging, my insecurities have fallen away. Imagine once being so scared of rejection that you wore make-up in bed. Now imagine that same woman feeling so loved that she no longer wears make-up at all.

I am loved in a way where I am truly accepted, by another human being *and* myself, and I adore it. It's moreish.

Postscript

The most important relationship any of us has post-divorce is the one with ourselves. I found my most authentic self through the veil of intense heartache. I wish the same discovery for each and every one of you reading this.

Divorce really can be the catalyst for positive change in our worlds.

About the Author

Holly won the *Good Housekeeping* best food blog award in 2016 for recipesfromanormalmum.com and has a recipe book published by Quadrille in the same name. She was also a finalist in the 2011 Great British Bake Off and runs a mail order brownie business mrsbellsbrownies.com. Her writing news and books can be found at hollybellbooks.com.

Holly has done many things for love. Highlights (and lowlights) include, but are not limited to, attending a Dr Who convention in Coventry, staying in a job three years too long, eating horse carpaccio (it was tough as old boots), listening to many a Green Day song crucified acoustically in a teenage bedroom, pretending to be ecstatic at receiving four dog-eared tea lights for Christmas, eating a full Irish breakfast prepared by a chain-smoking proprietor before daily hospital visits to her boyfriend in Ireland (he burst his hernia stitches on holiday...), typing up a play that would be his breakthrough work, taking a day off work to research sofas for his new flat at Chelsea Harbour without him, watching a Pink Floyd tribute band on an anniversary, throwing away a much loved ski jacket, keeping Coco Pops in her cupboard, pretending to like bone marrow salad, writing his sister's homework for her creative writing post grad, watching a Viking re-enactment, donating all her books because they were taking up too much room, dressing up in leather trousers and carrying a whip to promote a band (called Kinky...the whip was relevant) and ordering cannelloni every Saturday just because her baby son liked it.

Holly Bell is based in Leicester in the UK. She lives with her three sons, her boyfriend and a very disagreeable cat.

@hollybellmummy
@mrsbellsbrownies

The Nob List

See page 25 for an explanation. These are your pages to fill, if you feel it will help you.

The I Get To List

See page 187 for an explanation.

Thank You

To every single woman who has shared her story with me and given me permission to tell it.

To the many women who have held me up during a very difficult time. You know who you are.

To Gott Gott, my hand friend, for really believing in me and pushing me to write, even when I tried to find a playhouse to paint.

To my parents for all their support in innumerable ways.

To Lady V for her expert first reading, copy checking, perfect postscript and general cheering from the side lines. Who'd have thought that a meeting through ex-boyfriends at Clapham South tube station before Notting Hill Carnival would result in a friendship spanning decades? Your positivity is infectious.

To Sarah Greaves for *so* much, but not least giving up her Bank Holiday Monday to proofread.

To Sam O'Halloran for happily proofreading for me and being such a support in the darker days.

To the woman who wishes to remain uncredited, for giving up two days to proofread and copy edit. And for having expert eagle eyes!